The Best of *Bead&Button* Magazine

Polymer Pizzazz

27 Great Polymer Clay Jewelry Projects

Compiled by Kristin Schneidler

D0521704

© 2006 Kalmbach Trade Press. All rights reserved. This book may not be reproduced in part or in whole without written permission of the publisher, except in the case of brief quotations used in reviews. Published by Kalmbach Trade Press, a division of Kalmbach Publishing Co., 21027 Crossroads Circle, Waukesha, WI 53186. These books are distributed to the book trade by Watson-Guptill.

Printed in the United States of America

11 10 09 08 07   2 3 4 5

Publisher's Cataloging-In-Publication Data
(Prepared by The Donohue Group, Inc.)

Polymer pizzazz : 27 great polymer clay jewelry projects / compiled by Kristin Schneidler.

    p. : ill. ; cm.

    Best of Bead&Button magazine
    ISBN: 978-0-87116-236-6

1. Polymer clay craft--Handbooks, manuals, etc. 2. Jewelry making. I. Schneidler, Kristin. II. Title: 27 great polymer clay jewelry projects III. Title: Twenty-seven great polymer clay jewelry projects IV. Title: Best of Bead&Button magazine V. Title: Bead & Button.

TT297 .S36 2006
745.594/2

Acknowledgments: Laura Baird, Lisa Bergman, Mindy Brooks, Karin Buckingham, Jim Forbes, Jill Erickson, Lora Groszkiewicz, Kellie Jaeger, Carrie Jebe, Diane Jolie, Patti Keipe, Alice Korach, Pat Lantier, Tonya Limberg, Lisa Mooney, Debbie Nishihara, Dori Olmesdahl, Cheryl Phelan, Carole Ross, Salena Safranski, Maureen Schimmel, Kristin Schneidler, Lisa Schroeder, Mark Thompson, Terri Torbeck, Helene Tsigistras, Annette Wall, Elizabeth Weber, Bill Zuback

These designs are for your personal use. They are not intended for resale.

All projects have appeared previously in *Bead&Button* or *Art Jewelry* magazines.

CONTENTS

INTRODUCTION

When my children were young, I introduced them to a variety of crafts, and I joyfully recall many pleasant hours of laughter and delight as we played together around a table in the sunroom of our old house. One afternoon, a friend brought us a box of clay – not the familiar sticks of modeling clay we were used to, but squares of a malleable, brightly colored material that, when baked, hardened into a permanent shape. We loved how easy it was to work with, and we came up with endless new ideas of things to make.

That was my first exposure to polymer clay. And, although the clay proved to be an entertaining medium in the hands of my children, I never thought about its artistic potential. It wasn't until years later, when I started working at *Bead&Button* magazine, that I learned how remarkably versatile and sophisticated polymer clay can be.

The techniques for working with polymer clay are relatively simple: you knead the clay to make it pliable, blend colors to customize a palette, roll flat sheets or cylindrical logs to build shapes, and so on. The basics are easy to learn, yet they open up a world of creativity far beyond anything you might expect. You can give the clay the look of ivory, stone, porcelain, or wood; leave it matte or polish it to a high-gloss finish; carve it; transfer images to it; use it alone or combine it with other materials; or all of the above. Once you unwrap a package or two of polymer clay, you're free to explore in ways that few other art or craft media can offer.

The projects in *Polymer Pizzazz* represent the work of many of the country's finest teachers and artists in this medium. Page by page, you'll learn how to get started and how to expand your skills. We encourage you to experiment with the ideas presented here and to develop your own variations of the finished work. Let your imagination take charge. In no time, you'll be making beautiful pieces of jewelry and decorative items for your home with this remarkable, affordable material – polymer clay.

Mindy Brooks, editor
Bead&Button magazine

BASICS

This chapter presents an overview of polymer clay and the tools you can use with it to create beautiful jewelry. We've included tips on working with polymer clay, basic techniques used in almost any polymer-clay project, jewelry-making basics, and a glossary of polymer-clay terms.

POLYMER CLAY

What is polymer clay?

Polymer clay is a contemporary, synthetic, modeling compound made of polyvinyl chloride (PVC), pigments, and a plasticizer. The plasticizer keeps the clay pliable at room temperature. When heated, the molecular structure of the PVC stabilizes, and the clay hardens.

A toaster oven that is not used for food is a practical and safe appliance for baking, or curing, polymer clay. Bake according to the clay manufacturer's instructions.

A plethora of polymer products

Polymer clays differ a bit from brand to brand. In general, these differences fall into the categories of firmness, flexibility, strength, color, and opacity. When selecting polymer clay, choose a product that has the properties that most complement the requirements of your specific project. You may even experiment with combining two or more brands to achieve a custom result.

Liquid polymer clay, such as Liquid Sculpey, serves as an adhesive to bond raw clay to cured clay. It is available in both translucent and opaque formulas. It is an excellent agent for transferring images, or it can be tinted and applied as a glaze before curing.

Glazes are applied after curing to seal the finished work. Both Fimo and Sculpey include glazes in their product lines.

A softener, such as Sculpey Diluent, Kato Clear Medium, or Fimo Mix-Quick is blended with clay to help soften it during conditioning. It also acts as a bonding agent for uncured clay.

PRODUCT	MANUFACTURER	FEATURES	WEAKNESSES	BEST USES
Fimo	Eberhard Faber	Fimo is the first polymer clay to be marketed.	Can be challenging to condition.	Fimo is a durable clay that lends itself to many projects.
Fimo Classic	Eberhard Faber	Very firm.		Excellent choice for making canes.
Fimo Soft	Eberhard Faber	Some colors have glitter blended in.	Not as durable or strong as Fimo.	Easy to condition.
Sculpey	Polyform Products	Receives paint well.	Sculpey is softer and less durable than other formulations.	
Sculpey III	Polyform Products	Soft and easy to condition; appealing matte finish.	Translucent colors may "brown" if cured at too high a temperature.	
Sculpey Super Flex	Polyform Products	Very soft and remains flexible after baking.	A bit sticky when uncured.	Flexibility after baking makes it a good candidate for mold-making.
Premo Sculpey	Polyform Products	A sophisticated range of colors and pearl metallics. Easy to condition; remains strong and relatively flexible after curing.		
Super Sculpey	Polyform Products	Hard and strong clay.		Firmness makes Super Sculpey good for sculpting.
Cernit	T&F Kunststoffe	Very hard when cured; wide variety of flesh tones.	Elasticity makes it better for modeling than cane-making.	Formulated for doll makers.
Kato Polyclay	Van Aken International	Good general purpose product. Very firm.		Good for making canes.

TOOLS

Make certain that any tools, utensils, supplies, or appliances used for polymer clay become dedicated to the clay and are no longer used for food.

Use a **pasta machine** (**a**) to condition the clay and to roll pieces of clay into specific thicknesses.

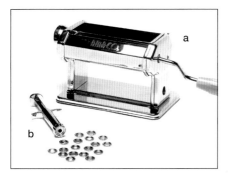

PASTA MACHINE SETTINGS

Settings on pasta machines vary. For example, Atlas machines have between seven and nine settings, with #1 being the thickest and #9 the thinnest. Amaco settings are the exact opposite – #1 is the thinnest and #7 is the thickest. It's a good idea to check the settings of your pasta machine so you have an approximate idea of the thickness you'll achieve with each setting.

An **extruder** (**b**) makes long, thin strands of clay. Different tips give the strands added texture and dimension.

Choose a smooth, durable work surface such as marble, a sheet of glass, or a smooth tile. To prevent clay from adhering to the work surface, experiment with working on parchment paper or freezer paper.

Use an **acrylic roller** (**c**) to flatten the clay. A **brayer** is a roller with a handle for added leverage or pressure.

Use a **burnishing tool**, a **bone folder** (**d**), or even the back side of a **spoon** to transfer an image from a transfer medium to polymer clay. Burnishing tools also will smooth and shine the clay.

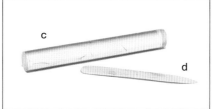

Cut polymer clay with a variety of **knives**. A craft knife, such as an **X-acto knife** (**e**), is handy for trimming clay, creating a beveled edge, or tracing a pattern. A **tissue blade** (**f**) is an extremely sharp, smooth, and flexible blade used for slicing canes and cutting thin and precise layers. A **Nu-Blade** is a brand of tissue blade developed and marketed by Donna Kato.

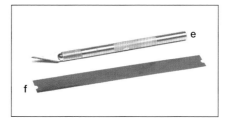

Safety Tip: Use a permanent marker to indicate the front and back of a blade. This prevents an injury caused by accidentally touching the cutting side.

Once clay is rolled and ready for use, a variety of **cutters** help make uniform shapes and sizes. **Kemper Kutters** create

precise, graduated sizes, but regular **cookie cutters** are equally useful. Be sure any utensils used for clay become dedicated to the clay.

Molds texture the clay and create a raised, or relief, image. **Soap molds** are ideal for this purpose. Additionally, you can use scrap polymer clay or a **mold-maker compound** to make a mold from any found object. Use a dry release, such as talc, on the mold so the clay casting will not stick.

Experiment with common items to texture your clay. **Carving and modeling tools, dental tools,** or even a small **sewing machine screwdriver** make unique marks in the clay. **Scratch** and **texture sheets** (**g**), a **kitchen scouring pad**, a **piece of screen** (**h**), or **rubber stamps** (**i**) also are useful for texturing. **Sculpting tools** (**j**) help with three-dimensional modeling.

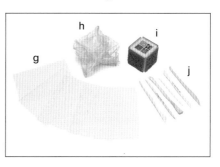

In addition to texture, you'll want to add color or pattern to your clay. Craft supplies such as **ink pads** (**k**), **paints, Prismacolor pencils,** and **decorating chalks** (**l**) will help you enhance your design. **Gold foil** (**m**) adds elegance. A **varnish** or **sealant** protects your image.

TOOLS

Once you've made a polymer clay pendant or bead, use a **needle tool** or **awl** to make a stringing hole. Or, punch a hole with a **drinking straw**. Drilling a hole in cured clay also is an option. Use a **drill** such as a **Dremel mini-mite**, a **spiral push drill**, or a **flex shaft**.

Bake polymer clay at a low temperature to set and harden. Rather than a pricey kiln, use a clay-dedicated **toaster** or **convection oven**. Be sure to check the accuracy of the oven's temperature with an **oven thermometer**. Bake clay on a smooth surface such as **card stock**.

Once cured, the finished piece may need a pinback or other embellishment, or it may become part of a larger project. **Cyanoacrylate glue** provides a superior bond. Its gel form is easier to control. Other brands designed for polymer clay use include Zap-A-Gap and Sobo.

Carve cured clay with **shaping tools** such as those designed for cutting linoleum.

While a clay piece can be used as soon as it cools from baking, additional polishing provides a high-quality finish. A **buffing wheel** is the easiest way to get the most professional results. If you don't have access to a buffing wheel, use **sandpaper** or a **sanding sponge**, beginning with 600 grit and progressing to finer grits. Sand your piece under water. (Very fine-grit sandpaper can be purchased at auto supply stores.) Hand polish with a **sturdy fabric** such as denim or polar fleece. Be sure to wear a **mask** when buffing, so you don't inhale any clay dust or particles.

Create beautiful jewelry with your polymer clay components using basic stringing and beading techniques.

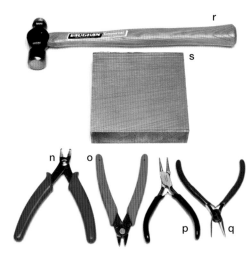

Jewelry tools, such as **crimping pliers (n)**; **diagonal wire cutters (o)**; **roundnose (p)** and **chainnose pliers (q)**; and a **ball peen hammer (r)** and **anvil (s)** will help you finish your jewelry. Jewelry-making techniques are detailed in the next section.

TECHNIQUES

Condition polymer clay

Conditioning polymer clay softens it and makes it easier to work with. All brands of polymer clay need some conditioning before you work with them, though the degree varies among brands and depends on whether the clay is from a newly opened package or left over from another project.

You can condition clay by hand or with

a pasta machine. To work it by hand, roll the clay into a ball, flatten it, then roll it into a snake. Fold the snake in half and roll it into a ball again. Continue making balls, snakes, and balls again until the clay is soft, pliable, and doesn't crack when folded.

If you use a pasta machine, most clay can be processed straight from the package. Adjust the machine to its thickest

setting, then flatten one end of the clay and roll it through the machine. If the clay breaks into small pieces, press the pieces together and run them through the machine again. A long sheet of clay will form. Fold it in half and put it through the machine, fold side first, so air will not become trapped between the pieces. If air pockets form, puncture them with a needle tool and run the clay through the machine again. Twenty or more passes may be necessary to condition the clay fully, but it's easier than kneading by hand.

To make conditioning even easier, try pre-warming the clay to make it softer. Some artists place the unopened package in their pocket or on a heating pad set to low heat. Or, use a clay-dedicated food processor to chop the clay into small pieces.

Many polymer-clay companies offer products that help soften the clay.

Once conditioned, roll out your desired thickness of clay using a pasta machine or by using playing cards and an acrylic roller.

Make a cane

Canes are formed by combining different colors and shapes of clay and rolling them into a cylinder. Cut a cane in halves or fourths and layer the sections together for a more complex pattern. Reduce the cane by hand-rolling and lengthening the cylinder. Some complex canes can begin with a diameter equal to a soda can, and then can be reduced to a diameter of an inch.

Avoid waste when you build a cane by keeping the ends trimmed throughout the

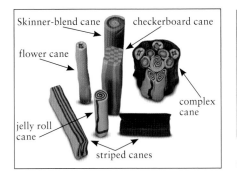

Skinner-blend cane   checkerboard cane

flower cane

jelly roll cane

striped canes

complex cane

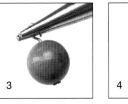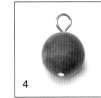

process. You'll still lose five to twenty percent from the ends because they do not display the pattern as well as the middle.

Polymer clay is temperature sensitive. After you've finished making a cane, the clay will be warm. Let the cane cool before slicing, either by resting it on your work-space or by placing it in the freezer for about 90 seconds.

Make a Skinner blend

Renowned polymer-clay artist Judith Skinner originated this method for making clay sheets with seamless color gradations.

1 Roll equal portions of two colors separately through the thickest setting of the pasta machine. The sheets will be roughly square or rectangular.

2 Fold the sheets in half diagonally (corner to corner).

3 Stack the sheets on top of one another, lining up the folded edges. Trim the rough edges so that the two sheets become right-angle triangles.

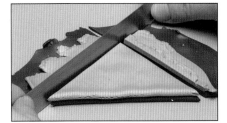

4 Separate the triangles and abut the diagonal (folded edge) sides with one another to form a square or rectangle. In order to create a sheet that contains unblended values of both colors, offset the placement slightly so that the corners do not meet. Trim the corners.

5 Roll the composite sheet through the pasta machine at the thickest setting.

6 Fold the sheet in half so the same colors meet (**below, left**). Roll the sheet through the pasta machine, folded edge first.

7 Continue to fold the sheet in the same direction and roll it through the machine until there are smooth gradations with no lines (**below, right**).

JEWELRY BASICS

Stringing and wire techniques

Plain loop

1 Trim the wire or head pin ⅜ in. (1cm) above the top bead. Make a right angle bend close to the bead.

2 Grab the wire's tip with roundnose pliers. The tip of the wire should be flush with the pliers. Roll the wire to form a half circle. Release the wire.

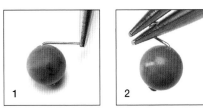

3 Reposition the pliers in the loop again and continue rolling.

4 The finished loop should form a centered circle above the bead.

Wrapped loop

1 Leave a 1¼-in. (3.2cm) wire tail. Grasp the wire with the tip of your chainnose pliers directly above the bead. Bend the wire (above the pliers) into a right angle.

2 Using roundnose pliers, position the jaws vertically in the bend.

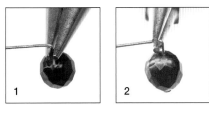

3 Bring the wire over the top jaw of the roundnose pliers.

4 Keep the jaws vertical and reposition the pliers' lower jaw snugly into the loop. Curve the wire downward around the bottom of the roundnose pliers. This is the first half of a wrapped loop.

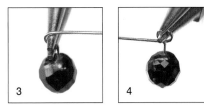

5 Position the chainnose pliers' jaws across the loop.

6 Wrap the wire around the stem, covering the stem between the loop and the top bead. Trim the excess wire and press the cut end close to the wraps with chainnose pliers.

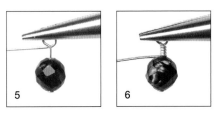

TECHNIQUES

Wrapping above a top-drilled bead

1 Center a top-drilled bead on a 3-in. (7.6cm) piece of wire. Bend each wire upward to form a squared-off U shape.
2 Cross the wires above the bead.

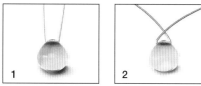

3 Using chainnose pliers, make a bend in each wire so the ends form a right angle.
4 Wrap the horizontal wire around the vertical wire as in a wrapped loop. Trim the excess wrapping wire.

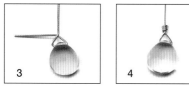

Flattened crimp

1 Hold the crimp using the tip of your chainnose pliers. Squeeze the pliers firmly to flatten the crimp.
2 Tug the wire to make sure the crimp is secure. If the wire slides, repeat the steps with a new crimp.

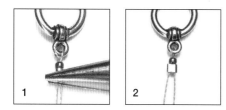

Folded crimp

1 Position the crimp bead in the notch closest to the crimping pliers' handle.
2 Separate the wires and squeeze the crimp.

3 Move the crimp into the notch at the pliers' tip and hold the crimp as shown. Squeeze the crimp bead, folding it in half at the indentation.
4 Test that the folded crimp is secure.

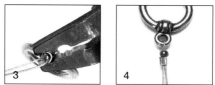

Surgeon's knot

Cross the right end over the left end and go through the loop. Go through again. Pull the ends to tighten. Cross the left end over the right end and go through once. Pull the ends to tighten.

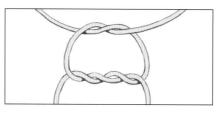

Bead tips

A bead tip hides the knots at the ends of a necklace or bracelet strung on cord. String a size 11º seed bead and tie the tail to the working thread with a square knot. String a bead tip so the two halves of the cup fit around the 11º. String the necklace or bracelet.

On the other end, string a bead tip, hinged end first, and an 11º. Tie the thread around the 11º with a square knot. Seal the knots with glue, and close the bead tips with chainnose pliers. Use roundnose pliers to roll the hooks around the loops of a clasp.

Glossary of Terms

cane: several clay snakes positioned lengthwise to create a design; when the cane is sliced horizontally, the pattern is revealed. Cane types: A jelly roll cane is made by layering flat clay sheets and tightly rolling them in a spiral; a bull's-eye cane is a thick snake wrapped with a thin clay sheet of clay; and a garbage cane is made of layers of small snakes and scraps of clay to make a larger, multi-colored and patterned snake.

condition: to prepare clay before use to make it more pliable, to remove air bubbles, and to make it stronger. Condition by hand kneading or by rolling through a pasta machine.

convection oven: an oven that heats using forced air circulation.

hydrophilic sponge: a sponge, used to apply paint or glazes to clay, that remains soft when dry. Similar to grout sponges sold in hardware stores.

inclusions: agents, including mica powders, spices, PearlEx powder, and ash, added to clay for imitative effects.

laminate: to superimpose layers of different materials onto one another.

latex or plastic gloves: types of gloves used by artists to prevent fingerprints from marring uncured clay.

loaf: a long, rectangular cane that will eventually be sliced.

marbleizing: combining two or more colors of clay to produce a pattern resembling marble.

mokume gane: a pattern resembling the age rings on a tree trunk, resulting from stacking thin layers of clay, then distorting, texturing, and slicing or carving through the layers to reveal colors.

reduction: shrinking a design to a smaller size without distortion, for example by rolling a cane.

Skinner blend: a method of folding and pressing colors of clay until they form a smooth gradation from one color to the next (by Judith Skinner, see p. 9).

snake or log: a cylinder made from a ball of clay, usually by rolling it between your hand and the work surface.

BEADS

Beautiful beads make beautiful jewelry. Whether you prefer a bold statement or a delicate design, you'll be amazed at the variety of results possible with polymer clay. Begin by making your own beads, and distinctive, signature jewelry will follow.

Modern marbling

The classic technique gets a new medium –
and a fresh new look

by **Karen and Ann Mitchell**

For several centuries, artists have produced swirling designs through a technique known as marbling: They floated inks or paints on water, then carefully laid paper down upon the water and lifted images off the liquid and onto the paper.

Reinvented for clay use, this marbling project eliminates the need for water. Instead, tinted liquid clay is the coloring medium, which glides over solid polymer-clay bases. Use skewers (or any finely pointed tool) to form feathered patterns, then bake the clay to set the marbleized colors. The process generates fluid designs baked onto clay beads – perfect

accents for a gemstone necklace or a simple earring set.

Prepare the bases

[1] Condition the copper clay (see Basics, p. 5). Roll the conditioned clay through the pasta machine to achieve a ¹⁄₁₆-in. (2mm) thickness. Cut the sheet in half and stack the two pieces. Use a brayer or an acrylic rod to press the sheets together, rolling from the center out to eliminate air pockets.

[2] Dip the cutters in cornstarch, then cut out five triangles, one large teardrop, four medium teardrops, and two small teardrops (**photo a**). Remove excess clay and save it for another project.

[3] Gently insert head pins into the teardrops, pushing up from the rounded end and through the pointed end, until the head of the pin is flush with the rounded end (**photo b**). Set the drops on a baking tray.

[4] Cut the 20-gauge wire into ten 1½-in. (3.8cm) pieces. Make wrapped loops (Basics) with five of the pieces. Trim each wrapped section to ³⁄₁₆ in. (5mm). Dab Translucent Liquid Sculpey (TLS) on one wrapped end (**photo c**). Use roundnose pliers to gently insert the ends of a wrapped loop into a triangle, leaving only the loop exposed. Repeat with the other four triangles.

[5] Preheat the oven to 275°F (130°C). Insert the remaining 1½-in. (3.8cm) wires through the bottom of the triangles, ⅛ in. (3mm) from the edge (**photo d**). Place them on the tray. Bake the triangles and teardrops at 275°F (130°C) for 20 minutes. Remove them from the oven and allow to cool completely on a flat surface.

Paint and embellish

[1] Squeeze ½ tsp. (2.5ml) of TLS into each of four wells in the palette. Add ⅛ tsp. of Pearl Ex Pigment Powder to the wells, placing a different color in each well. Mix completely using a wooden skewer.

[2] Pick up a small amount of the blue liquid clay with the skewer. On all five triangles, slowly draw an inverted blue V, starting from the looped tip and working outward. After applying the blue liquid clay, place the piece on a flat surface. Clean the skewer. Add a V of white liquid clay to each triangle. The white clay should touch the blue. For the teardrops, slowly draw blue lines around each outer edge. Add white lines next to the blue all the way around (**photo e**).

[3] Fill in the remaining space on each triangle with the red liquid clay. Clean the skewer and place it at the center of one triangle. Lightly drag the tip through the three colors of liquid clay toward the loop. Do not drag liquid over an edge. Continue dragging, creating a pattern (**photo f**). Do not clean the skewer between lines. Repeat with the other four triangles, cleaning the skewer before starting a new base.

[4] Fill in the remaining space on each teardrop with red liquid clay. Place the skewer at the center of one teardrop and drag lines outward (**photo f**). Repeat on all the teardrops, cleaning the skewer before starting a new base. If you smear the colors beyond what's aesthetically pleasing, remove all the

liquid clay from the base with a paper towel and start again.

[5] Clean the skewer and attach a pinch of scrap clay to the tip (**photo g**) to create a handy placement tool. Tap the top of one cabochon with the clay tip, which will cause it to stick to the clay. Position the cabochon over the

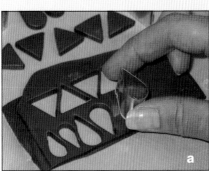

a

b

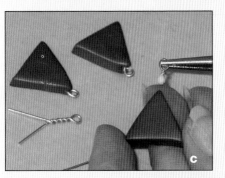

c

d

e

f

center of the large teardrop, ¼ in. (6.4mm) from the drop's bottom. Carefully place it and do not move it. Repeat on all teardrops, centering each cabochon about ⅛ in. from each bottom.

[6] Clean the skewer. Add a drop of copper liquid clay to the center of each triangle, layering over the red liquid clay but not the marbling. For each teardrop, put a dot of copper liquid clay directly above each cabochon (photo h). Drag the excess clay into a point toward the wire. Place all the triangles and teardrops on the tray and bake at 275°F (130°C) for 10 minutes. Allow the pieces to cool. Gently scrape any baked liquid clay off the loops. Finish all the pieces with Fimo Gloss Varnish and dry thoroughly.

[7] Remove the straight wires from the triangles. Make plain loops with the teardrops' head pins (Basics). Connect the triangle and teardrop loops (photo i), setting two medium drops aside for earrings.

Put it together

[1] Center the largest teardrop set on 20 in. (51cm) of beading wire. Add a seed bead, a medium teardrop set, a seed bead, a small teardrop set, and a seed bead (photo j). Then string an 8mm gemstone, a seed bead, a gemstone chip, and a seed bead. Repeat this four-stone pattern nine more times. String a crimp and a 4mm split ring. Go back through the crimp and the next few beads. Crimp the crimp bead (Basics) and cut the tail. To finish the other end, use the 3mm split ring instead of the 4mm. Open the ring (Basics), add the clasp, then close the ring. This necklace should be approximately 16 in. (41cm) long; add or remove an equal number of beads on each side to adjust the fit.

[2] For the earrings, open the plain loop on a teardrop, connect an earwire, and close the loop. Repeat for a second earring.

MATERIALS
- 2-oz. (56g) pkg. Premo Sculpey, copper
- 2 oz. (59ml) Translucent Liquid Sculpey
- Pearl Ex Pigment Powders: true blue, pearl white, red russet, and copper sparkle
- Fimo Varnish (mineral-based gloss)
- **20** 8mm gemstones: denim lapis lazuli, lapis lazuli, howlite, or sodalite
- **20** small gemstone chips, to match 8mm stones
- **7** 4–5mm stone cabochons, to match 8mm stones
- **46** size 6º seed beads or glass e-beads, topaz with ghost finish
- 10mm lobster clasp
- 15 in. (38cm) 20-gauge wire
- **7** 2-in. (5cm) head pins
- 4mm split ring
- 3mm split ring
- **2** crimp beads
- pair earring wires
- flexible beading wire, .014

TOOLS & SUPPLIES
- pasta machine*
- toaster or convection oven with oven thermometer*
- brayer or acrylic rod
- clay cutters (triangle: ⅝ x ¾ in.; teardrops: ⅞ x 1¼ in., ⁷⁄₁₆ x ⅞ in., ⁵⁄₁₆ x ⅝ in. Kemper Tools, 800-388-5367, kempertools.com)
- cornstarch
- flat baking tray*
- roundnose pliers
- wire cutters
- 4-well aluminum palette
- wooden skewer
- varnish brush

*Dedicated to nonfood use

Painterly polymer

Form fabulous focal
beads from polymer
clay and paint

by **Dotty McMillan**

BEADS

This project takes its fashion-forward cue from several fabric-painting techniques. Pearlescent paints are layered on polymer disks, then strung with accent beads for a dynamic necklace.

Make the polymer-clay beads

[1] Tape a 12-in. (30cm) piece of freezer or waxed paper to your work surface. Cut a sponge into three 1-in. (2.5cm) cubes. Condition all the clay (see Basics, p. 5) and roll half of it to about ⅛ in. (3mm) thick, the widest setting on most pasta machines (**photo a**).

[2] Pour a nickel-size portion of the darkest paint color onto a corner of the paper. Dab one of the sponges in the paint, then dab it onto another area of the paper or a paper towel to remove excess paint. Sponge the paint onto the surface of the sheet of clay (**photo b**). The coverage doesn't need to be

complete, so don't worry if you miss spots. Rinse the sponge in a bowl of water and let the paint layer dry.

[3] Repeat step 2 using your middle-value paint color and a dry sponge. Space this paint farther apart so the

darker color is still partially visible (**photo c**). Rinse the sponge and let this layer dry. Or, if you want to blend colors, dab on another layer while the second layer is still wet. Use your lightest paint color for the third layer (**photo d**). Let

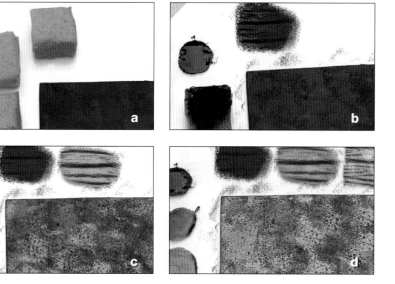

MATERIALS

necklace 34 in. (86cm)

- 4 2-oz. (56g) pkgs. Premo Sculpey, black
- Jacquard's Lumiere metallic paint or other acrylic fabric paint: light, medium, and dark colors
- Fimo Varnish (mineral-based gloss), Golden Polymer Varnish, or other gloss glaze
- 2 20 x 10mm beads
- 16 17 x 7mm glass beads
- 32 5mm glass beads
- 4 crimp beads
- flexible beading wire, .019

TOOLS & SUPPLIES

- pasta machine*
- toaster or convection oven*
- baking pan*
- freezer or waxed paper
- masking tape
- rubber stamp
- black ink pad
- hydrophilic sponge (also known as a grout sponge; purchase wherever tiling products are sold)
- glass bowl
- circle cutters, 1 in. (2.5cm) and ¾ in. (1.9cm)
- needle tool
- cardstock
- small paintbrush
- diagonal wire cutters
- crimping pliers

*Dedicated to nonfood use

---

the paint dry and rinse the sponge.

[4] Coat the rubber stamp with black ink. Stamp the pattern across the entire sheet of clay (**photo e**), carefully pressing down on the painted clay and lifting the stamp straight up so as not to smear the image. Let the ink dry.

[5] With the 1-in. (2.5cm) circle cutter, cut 28 circles (**photo f**). Set aside the excess painted clay scraps.

[6] Roll out the remaining, unpainted black polymer clay on the widest pasta machine setting to a thickness of approximately ⅛ in. (3mm). With a ¾-in. (1.9cm) circle cutter, cut 14 circles.

[7] Sandwich a black circle in the center between two painted circles, positioning the colored sides out; the edges will extend beyond the black interior. Press the edges together gently to form a smooth disk (**photo g**). Try not to remove paint. If it does lift off, dab the clay with

a small amount of any paint, then let it dry. Make a total of 14 disks.

[8] With the needle tool, carefully bore a hole in the rim of a clay disk. When you reach the center, stop. Remove the tool. Repeat on the other side to form a hole all the way through the disk (**photo h**). Repeat, making holes in all the disks.

[9] Set the clay beads on cardstock, place the cardstock on a tray in the toaster oven, and bake according to the manufacturer's directions. Let the beads cool. With a paintbrush, coat the beads with varnish. Let dry, then add a second coat.

String a necklace

These instructions are for a necklace 34 in. (86cm) long, but you may adjust the length as desired. Vary the colors, shapes, and sizes of the accent beads to add interest.

[1] On a 42-in. (1.1m) piece of flexible beading wire, string two 5mm beads, two crimp beads, and a 20 x 10mm bead.

[2] String a pattern of a polymer bead, a 5mm bead, a 17 x 7mm bead, and a 5mm bead (**photo i**) 14 times.

[3] String a 5mm bead, a 17 x 7mm bead, a 5mm bead, a 20 x 10mm bead,

two crimps, and a 17 x 7mm bead.

[4] Cross both wires and string each wire through the adjacent beads to the opposite crimp bead (**photo j**). Tighten the wires and beads, crimp the crimp beads (Basics), and trim the tails.

EDITOR'S NOTE:
For more fabric-painting inspiration, read Sherrill Kahn's *Creative Stamping with Mixed Media Techniques*, or visit impressmenow.com/books. htm.

Divided shield beads

Bold combinations harmonize in polymer-clay collars

by **Patricia Kimle**

These striking polymer-clay beads begin with a bead core that is textured and then gold-leafed. Next, each core is wrapped with two or more coordinating colors or patterns of clay, leaving a strip of the embellished core visible between them. It doesn't matter if the chosen elements are muted or vivid, simple or elaborate – the gold-leafed space that unites them makes almost every combination look sophisticated.

The beads shown in the step-by-step photos were made with a simple bull's-eye cane and a "garbage" cane embellished with translucent gold-leaf *mokume gane* overlays.

Make the bead cores

[1] Copy or trace the template or draw your own; feel free to adjust the size depending on whether you want larger or smaller shield elements. Cut out the template.

[2] Condition 3–4 oz. (85–113g) of scrap clay (see Basics, p. 5). Run it through the pasta machine on a medium setting until you have a long strip roughly 3 in. (7.6cm) wide, 14–16 in. (36–41cm) long, and ³⁄₃₂ in. (2.5mm) thick. Fold the strip in half lengthwise and roll with a brayer or an acrylic rod to thin and bevel the cut edge (**photo a**).

[3] Position the top of the shield template even with the folded edge and cut out the shape with a craft knife (**photo b**). Make 12–14 more bead cores.

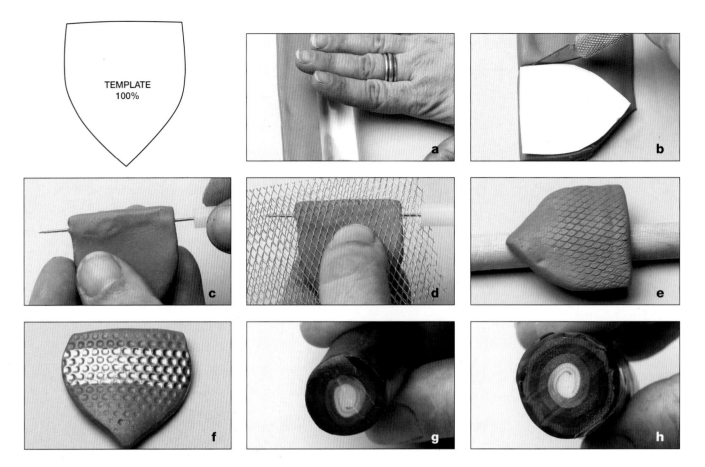

TEMPLATE
100%

[4] Smooth the edges of a bead core and pierce it with a needle tool about ⅛ in. (3mm) from the folded edge (**photo c**). While the needle tool is still inserted, press the core between two pieces of texture sheet, making sure to impress wherever the core will be exposed (**photo d**). If the sheet sticks to the clay, dust a little cornstarch on it before pressing. Peel away the texture sheet and remove the needle tool. Repeat with the other bead cores.

[5] With beads this large, a slight vertical curve helps them drape nicely around the neck and shoulders. Gently form the bead core into a slight curve. Lay it over a wood dowel (**photo e**) and place on a baking tray.

[6] Bake the bead cores according to the manufacturer's directions.

[7] After the bead cores have cooled, use a Krylon 18K Gold Leafing Pen to generously color the area you plan to expose between the pattern sheets in the next section (**photo f**).

Embellish the top of the bead cores

[1] Create a Skinner blend with black and pearl clay (Basics). Roll the sheet into a log with the pearl in the center (**photo g**).

[2] Blend a 3:1 ratio of copper clay to alizarin crimson clay. Roll a thin sheet of this blend in the pasta machine and wrap the log, slicing away the excess. Roll another thin sheet of black clay. Wrap the log with it (**photo h**).

[3] Reduce the cane until it is about 12 in. (30cm) long. Cut it into four equal pieces and stack and shape them into a square (**photo i**). Don't strive for a cane with even, equal sections; here, asymmetry makes for a more interesting, organic look. Reduce the cane again to a ½-in. (1.3cm) square.

[4] Roll a 3 x 4-in. (7.6 x 10cm) sheet of black clay through the pasta machine on a thin setting to get a sheet that is 1/16 in. (2mm) thick.

[5] Cut 1/16-in. slices of the cane and lay them next to each other on top of the sheet of black clay (**photo j**). Roll with a brayer or an acrylic rod to blend the seams, then run the sheet through the pasta machine on the thickest setting. Repeat, rolling the sheet at the next five settings consecutively. Rotate the sheet 90 degrees between each pass to keep the pattern from distorting.

[6] Cut the cane sheet into ½-in. (1.3cm) strips. Apply a small amount of Sculpey Diluent or Translucent Liquid Sculpey (TLS) to the top portion of the bead core. Wrap the cane sheet strip around the top of the core. Trim and fold the ends to fit, taking special care to keep a neat edge along the exposed core. Blend the seams (**photo k**) and re-pierce the hole. Repeat with the remaining bead cores.

[7] Bake according to the manufacturer's directions and cool.

Embellish the bottom of the bead cores

[1] Press the scraps from the previous cane together with 1 oz. (28g) of the excess red clay mix. Twist and roll the clay to create a marbled log. Shape it into a square cane.

[2] Roll a 3 x 4-in. (7.6 x 10cm) sheet of red clay through the pasta machine to create a 1/16-in. sheet.

[3] Repeat step 5 from the previous section using the square cane and red clay sheet you just made.

[4] To make the gold-leaf *mokume gane* for the overlay, use the pasta machine to roll 1 oz. of translucent clay

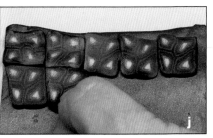

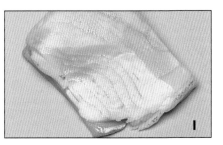

MATERIALS

- Premo Sculpey, one 2-oz. (56g) pkg. each of the following colors: alizarin crimson, copper, black, pearl, translucent
- 3–4 oz. (85–113g) scrap polymer clay
- Krylon 18K Gold Leafing Pen
- Sculpey Diluent or Translucent Liquid Sculpey (TLS)
- gold leaf (23K or composite)
- beading cord
- **2** seed beads
- **2** bead tips
- **18–20** 4mm gold-filled cylinder-shaped beads
- clasp

TOOLS & SUPPLIES

- pasta machine*
- toaster or convection oven*
- brayer or acrylic rod
- craft knife or tissue blade
- needle tool
- texture sheets or other patterning items
- cornstarch
- 1-in. diameter (2.5cm) wood dowel about 10 in. (25cm) long
- baking tray
- wet/dry sandpaper in 320-, 400-, and 600-grit
- water-based varnish
- roundnose pliers

*Dedicated to nonfood use

into a 4 x 4-in. (10 x 10cm) sheet, 1/16 in. thick. Apply the gold leaf and remove the carrier sheet. (Gold leaf is so fine it must be transferred by brush or paper – hence, the "carrier sheet." Discard the carrier sheet after transfer.) Cut the sheet into quarters and stack. Roll slightly with a brayer or an acrylic rod to crack and spread the leaf. Cut the stack in half and layer the halves again. Cut the stack in half diagonally from a top corner to the opposite bottom corner (creating two wedge shapes). Stack the bottom piece on the top. This should reveal an irregular stripe between the gold and translucent clay (**photo l**).

[5] Using a very sharp, clean blade, slice thin layers from the *mokume gane* block and apply them randomly to the marbled red sheet (**photo m**). Roll the sheet through the pasta machine until it is 1/16 in. (2mm) thick.

[6] Apply TLS or Sculpey Diluent to the bottom of a bead core. Cut two triangles from the cane sheet and position them on the bottom half of the core, abutting and smoothing the edges. Neatly trim the edge along the exposed core and blend the seams

(**photo n**). Repeat with the remaining bead cores.

[7] Bake the beads according to the manufacturer's directions.

Finish the beads

[1] Sand the beads with wet/dry sandpaper, beginning with 320-grit and progressing through 400- and 600-grit.

[2] Apply 2–3 coats of water-based varnish, drying between applications.

String the necklace

[1] Decide on the length of your necklace. This shape and size of bead works best at collar length. Measure your neckline, add 6 in. (15cm), and double this measurement. Cut a strand of beading cord to this length.

[2] Thread a needle to the center of the beading cord. String a seed bead 3 in. from the cord ends. Tie the tail and working thread over the bead with two or three surgeon's knots (Basics). Glue the knots, let them dry, and trim the tails. String a bead tip to enclose the seed bead and close the tip (Basics).

[3] String two or three gold-filled beads. Alternate shield beads and gold beads until you are 1/2 in. (1.3cm) from

the desired length. String two or three gold beads and a bead tip. Cut the needle from the cord. String a seed bead on one cord end, so it nestles in the bead tip. Tie the cord tails together over the bead with two or three surgeon's knots. Glue the knots, let them dry, and trim the tails. Close the bead tip.

[4] Use roundnose pliers to attach the bead-tip hooks to the clasp loops.

Filigree beads

Create polymer-clay magic with dissolving packing peanuts

by **Jody Bishel**

Cornstarch packing peanuts make an ecologically friendly choice for shipping needs, but they also make great temporary armatures for your polymer-clay projects. You can build shapes by moistening the peanuts and pressing them together, then forming clay around the shapes. After the clay is baked, you soak the piece in water and – voila! – the peanut dissolves, leaving an open space inside the baked clay.

This design takes the concept a step further by using a simple tube bead as an inner core, and wrapping it with a peanut to support an outer filigree design made of more clay. After the peanut is dissolved, the core can be glimpsed inside its cage.

Make the core tube beads

[1] Condition the clay (see Basics, p. 5). Roll the clay into a snake approximately 1½ in. (3.8cm) long and the diameter of your little finger. Skewer the snake lengthwise and roll the clay on the skewer until the tube is about 5/16 in. (8mm) in diameter. Slice the tube into 1¼-in. (3.2cm) lengths, but don't remove the beads from the skewer.

[2] Bake the tube beads following the manufacturer's directions, leaving the beads on the skewer during baking for support. When the tube beads have cooled, remove all but one tube from the skewer.

Make a centered spiral bead

[1] Prepare the cornstarch peanuts by

pinching them between your fingers and rolling them back and forth between thumb and forefinger. This compresses the peanut and will make it easier to work with. Wrap a tube bead with a peanut and secure the end by moistening the peanut with water and pressing it to itself (**photo a**). The number of peanuts you use depends on their length and density (one and one-half peanuts were used to wrap the tubes shown in this project). Check that the bead is evenly wrapped by looking lengthwise down the bead. Leave about ¼ in. (6mm) of tube bead exposed on each end.

[2] Roll out a sheet of clay with a pasta machine so it is 1/16 in. (2mm) thick. With the dull side of the tissue blade, mark but don't cut the sheet into strips ⅛ in. (3mm) wide by 1½ in. (3.8cm) long. (Each bead uses four strips, so calculate the number of centered spiral beads you want and mark the appropriate number of strips.) Decorate the strips by pressing designs in the clay with dental tools, small texturing tools, a ball-ended tool, or a tiny screwdriver. Cut the strips apart when you've finished decorating them.

[3] Brush a little Translucent Liquid Sculpey (TLS) or Sculpey Diluent on the exposed tube bead to help the raw clay stick. Place a strip across the cornstarch peanut wrapping and press the ends against the tube. Trim off any extra clay. Turn the bead and attach another strip directly opposite from the first one. Repeat with two more strips to divide the bead into quarters (**photo b**). Check to see that the bead is balanced by looking down its length on the skewer. If you're new to polymer clay, stop and bake the bead now according to the manufacturer's directions. Otherwise, if you feel confident with your skills, proceed to the next step and continue decorating your bead.

THE RIGHT PEANUT:
Cornstarch packing peanuts are not nearly as common as their more ubiquitous counterpart, Styrofoam peanuts. Don't substitute Styrofoam peanuts for cornstarch peanuts! When baked, Styrofoam will melt and make a gooey mess or possibly even catch fire inside your oven. Cornstarch peanuts are water soluble. Verify that your packing peanuts are indeed made of cornstarch by placing one in water to see that it dissolves. Stockpile any cornstarch peanuts you receive in the mail for future projects.

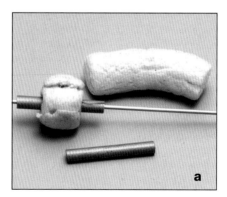

a

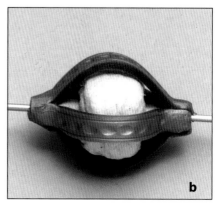

b

MATERIALS

- 2-oz. (56g) pkg. Premo Sculpey, any color
- cornstarch packing peanuts (available at office supply and packing supply shops)
- Translucent Liquid Sculpey (TLS) or Sculpey Diluent

TOOLS & SUPPLIES

- pasta machine*
- toaster or convection oven*
- metal skewer (thin knitting needle or steel music wire available at hobby shops)
- craft knife or tissue blade
- dental tools
- small texturing tools
- ball-ended tool
- tiny screwdriver (for repairing glasses or sewing machines)

*Dedicated to nonfood use

Additional variations

Instructions for three basic variations on the filigree bead are presented here, but the design is limited only by your imagination. For example, instead of a plain tube bead for your core, you can make a spiral central tube by stacking sheets of clay to the desired thickness and cutting them into a squared bead length. Carefully push the clay onto the skewer and twist it to make the spiral.

You can vary the spiral cage bead by attaching the twisted strips at a slight angle. This will give a greater impression of motion, at the price of some symmetry. (The other beads presented here rely on uniform placement of their elements and do not lend themselves to this variation.)

To create matching components, make earrings and pendants by working with a bead at the end of the skewer so that the bottom cap can be tapered to a point with no opening. Embed a telephone wire loop in the opposite end for hanging.

Once you have mastered making beads, you can adapt the design to a larger scale to make filigree holiday ornaments or toys. For added strength with larger pieces, insert a piece of steel music wire where the hole would be and cover it completely with the clay. The dreidel shown below is one example of a large-scale version.

[4] Make four ½-in.-diameter (1.3cm) spirals by rolling slender snakes of clay with tapered ends and coiling them. Attach each spiral by moistening it with TLS and pressing it in place, overlapping onto the vertical strips slightly (photo c). Cap the bead by sliding ⅜-in. (1cm) balls of clay down both ends of the skewer and pressing them around the ends of the tube bead. Smooth out the balls and decorate them with dental tools (photo c). (Photo c shows one finished end and the other end awaiting decoration.) Repeat to make the desired number of centered spiral beads.

[5] Bake the beads according to the manufacturer's directions. After they are done, immerse the beads in warm water to dissolve the peanut armature. You may have to prod partly dissolved bits out of tight corners to complete the process.

Make a leaf bead

[1] Take one of your tube beads and follow steps 1–3 for the centered spiral bead.

[2] Make eight ⅜-in.-long (1cm) leaf shapes. Moisten the base of each leaf with TLS and press them into place between the vertical strips at each end. Cap the ends with ⅜-in. balls of clay as in step 4 above. Once the leaves and balls are attached, add vein lines to the leaves and decorate the bead caps (photo d).

[3] Finish the bead as in step 5.

Make a spiral cage bead

[1] Take one of your premade tube beads and follow step 1 for the centered spiral bead to prepare a spiral cage bead.

[2] Cut eight strips of clay 2 in. (5cm) long by ³⁄₁₆ in. (5mm) wide and thick. Moisten the ends of the tube bead with a little TLS. Gently twist a strip and lay it over the cornstarch peanuts, pressing the ends against the tube bead (photo e). Trim off any extra length. Repeat with the remaining strips. Cap the ends with ⅜-in. (1cm) balls of clay.

[3] Finish the bead as in step 5.

Grand illusions

Create mysterious images on polished polymer-clay beads

by **Grant Diffendaffer**

The first thing you notice when you take a good look at this intriguing bead is its texture. Actually, this technique involves removing texture, which not only leaves behind interesting designs, but also creates the illusion of depth. The sparkling color shifts aren't caused by paints or glazes. Instead, blending the clay creates the color variation, and the alignment of pearlescent flakes, called micas, produces the shimmer from within the clay itself.

This project builds on techniques introduced by Mike Buessler, Pier Voulkos, and other polymer-clay pioneers, and adds a number of refinements to help you achieve a significant visual impact with the clay.

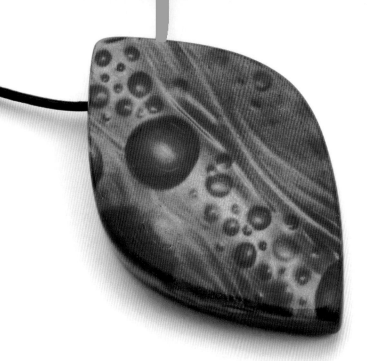

MATERIALS
- Premo Sculpey, 2-oz. (56g) pkg. of one of the following colors: blue pearl, red pearl, or green pearl
- 3 2-oz. (56g) pkgs. Premo Sculpey, gold pearl

TOOLS & SUPPLIES
- pasta machine*
- toaster or convection oven*
- tissue blade
- 2 ⁵⁄₁₆-in. (8mm) spacers, at least 6 in. (15cm) long
- 2 texture stamps (see "Texture Stamps for Polymer Clay," p. 26)
- wet/dry sandpaper in 800-, 1000-, 1200-, and 1500-grits
- buffing wheel
- spiral push drill (micromark.com, item #26101)
- flex shaft and drill bits: ¹⁄₆₄-, ¹⁄₃₂-, ³⁄₆₄-, ¹⁄₁₆-, ⁵⁄₆₄-, ³⁄₃₂-, ⁷⁄₆₄-, and ¹⁄₈-in. (.5, .8, 1.2, 1.5, 2, 2.4, 2.8, 3mm)

*Dedicated to nonfood use

Use the Skinner blend method to combine red pearl with gold clay or blue pearl with gold. You may want to practice with only one color. For the strongest, single-color shimmer (or mica shift) use gold clay.

Prepare the clay
[1] Condition a package of blue pearl clay (see Basics, p. 5). Cut the clay to a 4 x 5-in. (10 x 13cm) rectangle. Repeat, using a package of gold clay (**photo a**).
[2] Cut the rectangles on a diagonal and make pairs with alternating colors (**photo b**).
[3] Stack one pair on top of the other (**photo c**). Blend the clay in the pasta machine using the Skinner blend method (Basics). If you are pleased with your color results, skip to step 6. If you wish to reduce the contrast of

the blend, continue with the next step.
[4] Trim the clay to a 5½ x 10½-in. (14 x 26.7cm) rectangle, then cut into three equal rectangles (**photo d**).
[5] Stack the rectangles with the colors aligned (**photo e**). Place the gold end in the pasta machine and run the stack though so it is ¹⁄₁₆ in. (2mm) thick.
[6] Trim the gold end, then roll the

POWER TOOLS: If using power tools to make a stringing hole makes you uncomfortable, create a stringing hole before baking the clay. Twist a needle tool into one side, then the other. The result is less polished, but still functional.

clay into a cane, starting at the trimmed end. Be careful not to trap air bubbles. Rock the clay back and forth, reducing it to about 1 in. (2.5cm) in diameter. Trim the ends and cut it into two 3-in. (7.6cm) sections (**photo f**).
[7] Mark two parallel lines that are ⁹⁄₁₆ in. (1.4cm) apart, then slice through the clay along the lines (**photo g**).

Add texture
You will use stamps to create texture in this project. The ideal stamp is deeply cut, packed with detail, and somewhat rigid, so when you press down, the clay gives way rather than the stamp. For stamp options, see "Texture Stamps for Polymer Clay," p. 26.
[1] Wet the stamps thoroughly using a soft toothbrush to moisten all the crevices. Place one stamp face up on

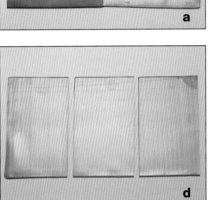

a

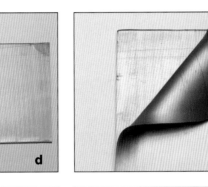

b

c

d

e

f

g

h

i

your work surface, then top with spacers. Paint stir sticks are used in the project shown, but you can also use rulers, stiff cardboard, or stacked playing cards.

[2] Wet the clay and position it between the spacers. Place the second stamp on top of the clay (**photo h**).

[3] Press the top stamp down with a board or a hardback book until the spacers prevent you from pressing down any more.

[4] Gently separate the stamps, taking care not to stretch the clay. If it sticks, pull the clay carefully away, one edge at a time. Gently pat the clay dry with a paper towel.

[5] Trim the texture off the surface of the clay, cutting just above the depth of the impressions. To do so, place the clay on a flat surface and saw gently

back and forth with a tissue blade. Don't cut too deeply; a later sanding removes the remaining texture.

[6] Cut the clay into the desired shape. For curves, bend a tissue blade and make two even cuts (**photo i**).

[7] Place the clay pieces in the oven and bake according to the manufacturer's directions. (These beads were baked at 275°F/135°C for 30 minutes.) Let the pieces cool in the oven to guard against cracking.

Finish the bead

[1] Wet a sheet of 800-grit sandpaper and a cooled bead. Place the piece on top of the sandpaper.

[2] Sand the bead against the paper with back-and-forth motions. Rinse the bead and sandpaper frequently. For curved edges, roll the edge against

the paper as you draw the bead toward you (**photo j**). For a mirror-smooth finish, repeat with 1000-grit, 1200-grit, and 1500-grit sandpaper. For softer, more rounded edges, place a wet sponge under the sandpaper.

[3] Buff gently with a buffing wheel; wear eye protection. (If you don't have a buffing machine, you can use a

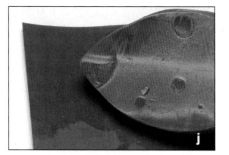

EDITOR'S NOTE:
A spiral push drill is a hand-powered drill. Push steadily and gently in an up-and-down manner and take your time; if you press too hard, you may break the bit. If you don't have a spiral push drill, try alternating between a needle tool and a round needle file, or see "Power Tools," p. 24.

wheel mounted on a drill press. The wheel used in this project is for buffing cars and is made of polyester rather than cotton. If you use a muslin wheel, choose the unsewn variety.) If you don't have access to power tools or prefer not to use them, you can buff by hand with soft cloths, though you will not achieve the same level of polish.

[4] Mark where you want the stringing hole, using a pencil or needle tool. With a spiral push drill and a 1/64-in. (.4mm) bit, drill one side and then the other until your holes meet (**photo k**). See Editor's note, above.

[5] Using a flex shaft or power drill, enlarge the hole with a 1/32-in. (.8mm) bit. Gradually increase the size of the bit until the hole is 1/8 in. (3mm) or your desired size.

Texture stamps for polymer clay

There are four great options for creating texture in polymer clay:
- Purchase commercially available rubber stamps or texture plates
- Make rubber stamps (granthams.com)
- Design "plate and matrix" stamps (readystamps.com)
- Make polymer-clay stamp plates.

This last option requires some practice, but offers immense satisfaction. Since the surface of a clay stamp isn't perfectly even, however, it's easy to lose detail in the finished work. Try a bold pattern like the one shown below; reduce or enlarge the image as you desire. To make your own polymer-clay stamps, follow these directions:

[1] Roll out 10 oz. (284g) of scrap polymer clay on the thickest pasta machine setting.

[2] Fold it over to make two 5 x 5-in. (13 x 13cm) sheets of double thickness.

[3] Cut several holes with small clay cutters. Poke more holes with straws of various sizes, a ball stylus, and other texture tools. Gently smooth all ridges with your fingers, a brayer, or an acrylic rod and make sure that the surface is as evenly flat as possible. Leave some space untextured to carve later.

[4] Bake the polymer clay at 275°F (135°C) for 30 minutes.

[5] After the clay cools, use a linoleum cutter to carve additional designs.

TOOLS & SUPPLIES
- 10 oz. (284g) scrap polymer clay
- Kemper or other clay cutters
- ball stylus
- texturing tools (straws, pens, nails, etc.)
- brayer or acrylic rod (optional)
- Speedball linoleum cutter with V blades
- toaster or convection oven dedicated to nonfood use

Warring States beads

One of China's ancient bead designs is beautifully re-created in polymer clay

by **Lura Hatcher**

This polymer-clay version was inspired by glass beadmaker Dan Adams' Warring States beads, which in turn took their inspiration from the original source: ancient China's Warring States glass beads. This remarkable period in China (roughly 481–221 B.C.) was a time of extreme tumult, with many regional warlords struggling to annex smaller states around them and thus rise to power. Despite the chaos, great technological strides were made, including the switch from primitive bronzeworking to more modern

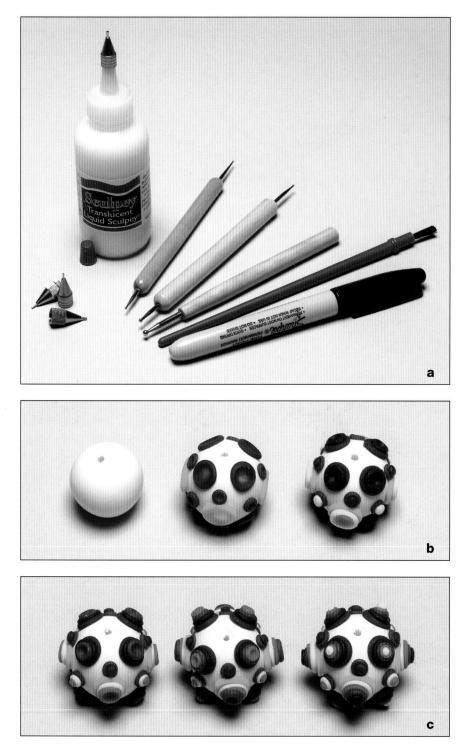

ironworking. Trade developed between states and countries, leading to exchanges of ideas and information.

Among the Chinese, glass beads were seldom worn, being instead a valuable trading commodity. With its multiple protrusions of different sizes and layers (called "horns"), the Warring States bead is a complex creation, and no one really knows how or why these beads came into being. Whatever their origin or medium, Warring States beads are a time-consuming creation, but the results are striking and well worth the effort.

The instructions presented here are for the rainbow beads. The tangerine beads are made by mixing various shades of orange and yellow polymer clay. Adding a little black when making the horns will help the colors pop. Don't restrict yourself to just spheres; this technique also translates well to other shapes, including squares, triangles, and dumbbells.

Make the basic beads

[1] Condition the entire packet of white Sculpey III clay (see Basics, p. 5) and roll it into a cylinder with a circumference about the size of the bead you want. Slice the cylinder into even sections, but make half of the sections wider than the other half, which will produce two different types of beads. Shape the larger sections into ¾-in. (1.9cm) round beads and the smaller sections into disc-shaped beads ⅝ × ⅜ in. (1.6 × 1cm).

[2] Pierce the bead shapes with a needle tool or awl, entering the hole from both ends to smooth the edges. Bake according to the manufacturer's directions. (The beads in this project were baked at 265°F/130°C for 20 minutes.)

[3] While the beads are baking, condition the other colors of clay and work a small amount of translucent Fimo into each color, using a ratio of two parts Sculpey III to one part translucent Fimo. Fimo is a stronger, more durable but less workable clay than Sculpey III; by mixing the two you add strength to the softer Sculpey III without altering its color. Work the clays until the Fimo is completely integrated. Now roll several

snakes in each color, ranging in widths from ⅛ to ¼ in. (3–6mm).

Add the horns

[1] Practice making horns – the bumpy knobs protruding from these beads – on your work surface. Line up four or more snakes in gradated widths, largest to smallest, and cut evenly across them, making slices approximately ¹⁄₁₆ in. (2mm) thick. Roll the slices into balls. Cut and roll more slices, making sure you're using the same amount of clay from one layer in a horn to the next so the horns match.

[2] Begin with the largest ball and press it gently against your work surface with a tool or your finger, leaving a dish-shaped indentation. Add the next smallest size ball and repeat the indentation process; continue with the next two layers. You may want to test different styluses or other implements (including your fingers) when pressing the balls of clay. Each layer must be pressed individually, leaving a concave indentation for the next ball of clay. It's helpful to jot down notes so you can repeat a particular effect accurately. When you are satisfied with the look of your horns, you are ready to begin making them on the beads.

[3] After the base beads are baked and cooled, sand them lightly to remove imperfections. Polish the beads with a soft cotton cloth to remove dust, which could hamper the application of the horns.

[4] Stake the blunt end of a bamboo skewer into a lump of unbaked clay and place the bead on the skewer point. This frees both hands for applying the horns. As you gain confidence in the process, you may want to hold the bead for better control while applying the horns. An inexpensive pair of tweezers with the ends bent inward can be used to clip into the bead holes.

[5] The first layer of every horn must be applied with Translucent Liquid Sculpey (TLS). This ensures the new clay will adhere securely to the baked clay. However, too much TLS leaves obvious glue spots on the bead. A craft tip set helps you regulate the amount of

TLS applied. Attach one of the small metal tips directly over the plastic tip on the TLS bottle (**photo a**). Subsequent horn layers do not require TLS, with the exception of the final ball.

[6] Apply the horns in sets of four, dividing the bead into quadrangles. Take four slices from the largest snake and roll them into balls. The largest horns on the sample bead started with a green layer. Put a small dab of TLS on the side of the bead and press a ball of clay over it, pushing gently with your finger or an implement. Apply the next green ball to the bead directly opposite the first. Press on the third and fourth balls between the first two balls. These green balls are pressed into circles about ⁵⁄₁₆ in. (8mm) in diameter. Check the bead from the top to ensure the placements are symmetrical. Position the smaller blue and red horn starts in sets of four, spacing them evenly around the bead (**photo b**).

[7] Apply each horn's subsequent layers, using gradually smaller balls of clay and implements (**photo c**). The smoothness of a metal stylus will enhance the application, allowing you to widen the clay gently to the right size circle as needed. Avoid wooden tools, which have a tendency to grab the clay.

[8] You can end a horn with an indentation or cap it with a very small ball of clay. Pushing in a ball can distort it, but without some pressure, the ball will not attach securely. Solve this problem by putting a tiny spot of TLS in the last concave circle before attaching the ball.

[9] After applying the horns, stake the beads on bamboo skewers baked into a base of clay or strung on a mandrel suspended over a shallow baking pan to prevent damage to the horns. Bake the beads according to manufacturer's directions. (These were baked at 265°F/130°C for 20–30 minutes.)

MATERIALS

- Sculpey III, 2-oz. (56g) pkg. each of the following colors: white, blue, fluorescent green, red-hot red, and atomic orange
- 2-oz. (56g) pkg. Fimo, translucent
- Translucent Liquid Sculpey (TLS)

TOOLS & SUPPLIES

- pasta machine*
- toaster or convection oven*
- craft knife or tissue blade
- needle tool or awl
- wet/dry sandpaper, 600- or 800-grit
- surgeon's mask
- bamboo skewers
- tweezers (optional)
- various sizes of styluses and/or round-ended paintbrushes, pencils, or pens
- craft tip set

*Dedicated to nonfood use only

EDITOR'S NOTE: In any project that requires sanding polymer clay, wear a mask to prevent breathing in the small particles of clay released during sanding.

Grapevine beads

Achieve the look of lampwork glass with TLS and a little heat

by **Carly Seibel**

Lampwork glass beads are the darling of the jewelry world, but can be expensive. Not many of us have the know-how and equipment to wield fire and glass to make our own. Polymer clay does such an amazing job of mimicking other materials, so why should lampworked glass be any different? The answer is: It isn't. By using some basic lampwork techniques, Translucent Liquid Sculpey (TLS), and the right temperature, you can create polymer-clay beads featuring the three-dimensional quality the best lampwork has to offer.

Lampworked beads are essentially layers of glass melted around a mandrel, with dots of glass melted on top to form brilliant patterns. The closest thing to glass stringer – the colored glass used to create raised patterns in lampwork glass – in polymer clay is TLS. But liquid clay tends to spread out when it's applied to cooled clay, which defeats the purpose of trying to achieve a raised surface embellishment. Here's where temperature makes all the difference: Working with hot beads makes the TLS set immediately upon application, allowing layers to build up.

> **EDITOR'S NOTE:** Work in a well-ventilated area since you will be curing the TLS at relatively high temperatures and the fumes can be somewhat noxious.

Mix the colors

[1] Squeeze or pour small amounts of TLS in the paint containers. Do not add any Sculpey Diluent because you want the TLS to be thick.
[2] Either select oil paints in the colors you want or mix primary colors to create two greens (one light and one dark), a purple, and a lavender.
[3] Tint each container of TLS with a tiny bit of one shade of oil paint. Only a small amount is needed to color the TLS.

Make the base beads

[1] Condition the black polymer clay (see Basics, p. 5). Using the pasta machine, roll out a sheet of clay about ⅟₁₆ in. (2mm) thick.
[2] Place the clay sheet on waxed paper to protect your work surface. Use a small brush to paint the clay's surface with the metallic champagne gold and metallic purple acrylic paints. Blend and swirl the colors together to create a marbleized effect (**photo a**).
[3] Before the paint dries, sprinkle a pinch of fine glitter across the sheet. Set the sheet aside to dry at least 15 minutes.
[4] While the paint dries, condition the scrap clay. Divide and roll the clay into balls; your finished bead should be approximately 30mm, so make the core a bit smaller. If you want to make a series of beads the same size, roll a log of clay, divide the log into equal sections, and roll each section into a ball.
[5] After the paint dries, roll over it

with a brayer or an acrylic roller to crack the paint and to add interest. Don't stretch the clay too much, however, or you will lose the metallic paint's shimmer.
[6] Tear or cut a piece of the painted sheet of clay and wrap it around one of the balls of scrap clay. Cover the ball completely, taking care to press out any air bubbles. Roll the ball in your hand to smooth the seams (**photo b**). Repeat this step with the remaining balls.
[7] Shape the clay balls into barrel, flattened oval, or round shapes. Use a smooth flat surface, such as a ceramic tile, to press the barrel shapes into flattened ovals.
[8] Use a needle tool to pierce a hole in each bead. Re-pierce from the

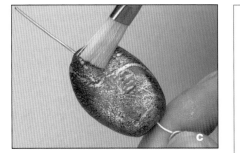

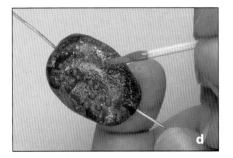

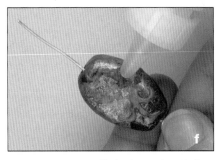

Protect your hands from hot beads by wearing gloves or using a pot holder.

MATERIALS

- oil paints: light and dark green, purple, and lavender (or choose primary colors such as blue, yellow, red, and white to custom-mix your own colors)
- Translucent Liquid Sculpey (TLS)
- ½ oz. (14g) Premo Sculpey, black
- acrylic paint: metallic champagne gold and metallic purple
- gold or silver glitter, very fine*
- scrap polymer clay
- Varathane Diamond Wood Finish (water-based)

TOOLS & SUPPLIES

- pasta machine**
- toaster or convection oven**
- 4 small paint containers with lids
- waxed paper
- brayer or acrylic rod
- ceramic tile or other flat object (optional)
- needle tool
- metal bead skewers
- shallow baking pan**
- ½-in. (1.3cm) flat paintbrush
- pot holder or oven mitt
- toothpicks
- squeeze bottle
- rubbing alcohol
- cotton balls
- craft knife

*If you cannot find very fine glitter, use a mortar and pestle to grind glitter to the necessary fineness.
**Dedicated to nonfood use

opposite direction to smooth the hole. [9] Place the beads on metal skewers and lay the skewers across a shallow baking pan with the skewers resting on the pan's edges so the beads do not touch the pan's surface. (If they aren't supported in this fashion, the beads will slump slightly in the oven and be lopsided.) Bake them according to the manufacturer's directions.
[10] After the beads have cooled, remove all but one bead from a skewer. Coat this bead with a layer of TLS, using a ½-in. (1.3cm) flat brush (**photo c**). Avoid putting too much TLS around the hole ends.
[11] Bake at 300°F (150°C) for 10 minutes. Leave the oven on.

Add the grape and vine design

[1] Remove the bead from the oven. Hold the skewer in your nondominant hand with an oven mitt or pot holder. Dip a toothpick in the purple TLS mixture and quickly dab on grape clusters as you twirl the skewer (**photo d**). Pick up small amounts of TLS as needed. Use a second toothpick to clean up stray drips. Place the bead back in the warm oven for three to five minutes to keep the bead hot and set the liquid clay.
[2] Remove the bead from the oven and use the light green TLS mixture to

apply vines to connect grape clusters (**photo e**). Drag the toothpick in swirls around the bead. Use the dark green to dab a few leaves on the vines. Return the bead to the oven for three to five minutes.
[3] Use the lavender TLS mixture to dab highlights on the purple grapes, then return the bead to the oven for five minutes.
[4] Remove the bead from the oven and use the squeeze bottle to trace over your grapes, vines, and leaves with untinted TLS (**photo f**). This step adds the extra dimension and translucence of lampwork to the design. Return the bead to the hot oven and bake for 15 minutes to thoroughly cure the liquid clay. Monitor the baking carefully to be sure the bead doesn't scorch; turn the skewer if necessary.
[5] Let the bead cool. Use a cotton ball with rubbing alcohol to wipe off any greasy residue on the bead. Making sure the flat brush you used in step 10 above is clean, coat the bead with a water-based finish such as Flecto's Varathane Diamond Wood Finish, blowing out any air bubbles. When it dries, apply a second coat. Clean up any accumulated sealant at the holes with a craft blade.

String the grapevine necklace

Your faux lampwork bead can be strung on a cord for a simple pendant. But if you'd like something fancier, follow these directions for making a beaded strand. Refer to Basics, p. 5, if you are unfamiliar with any techniques.

Make the grape cluster

[1] Cut a 30-in. (76cm) length of flexible beading wire. String a purple 11º seed bead to the center of the wire.

[2] String eight 6º seed beads over both wire ends.

[3] Thread a needle with 1 yd. (.9m) of purple Nymo. String a purple 11º seed bead to 8 in. (20cm) from the end. Sew through the bead again in the same direction.

[4] Sew into the 6º beads in the strand's middle and out the first 6º strung.

[5] Pick up two 11º beads, a teardrop, and two 11ºs and sew back into the first 6º bead strung, exiting the second 6º [**figure 1**].

[6] *Pick up three 11ºs, a teardrop, and one 11º** and sew up into the first 6º, exiting the third 6º [**figure 2**].

[7] Repeat * to ** from step 6 and sew up into the second 6º bead and out the fourth. Repeat the pattern to move up the strand adding grape fringes.

[8] After sewing out the eighth bead, repeat * to ** from step 6 and sew up into the sixth 6º bead strung and out the seventh bead. Repeat * to ** again, sewing into the fifth bead and out the sixth.

[9] Repeat the pattern in step 8 to move down the strand, adding more grape fringes.

[10] Sew up the strand and out the eighth bead, pick up three green 11º beads, a leaf bead, and three green 11ºs. Sew back through the eighth bead again. Repeat to add a second leaf fringe.

[11] Sew through the beads and tie a few half-hitch knots between beads to secure the thread. Glue the knots and trim the thread.

[12] Thread a needle to the starting tail and finish the thread as in step 11.

String the necklace

[1] String a gold-tone spacer, a green rondelle, the grapevine bead, a rondelle, a spacer, and an 8mm faceted glass bead over both wire ends.

[2] String 9 in. (23cm) of lavender 6º seed beads onto each wire end.

[3] Use clips to secure the beads on the wire temporarily.

[4] Thread a needle with 4 yd. (3.7m) of Nymo, doubled; add a stopper bead as in step 3 of "Make the grape cluster."

[5] Sew into the strand three to four beads from the last bead and out the next-to-last bead.

[6] Pick up *two green 11ºs, two purple 11ºs, one lilac 6º, two purple 11ºs, and two green 11ºs**. Count down four beads on the strand, then sew back up the strand to exit the bead before the bead last exited [**figure 3**].

[7] Repeat step 6, adding spiral fringe to the first 3 in. (7.6cm) of the strand.

[8] Replace * to ** from step 6 with two green 11º beads, two purple 11º beads, one magatama bead, one lilac 6º bead, one magatama bead, two purple 11ºs, and two green 11ºs for the next 4 in. (10cm) of the strand.

[9] About 2 in. (5cm) from the centerpiece, replace the lilac 6º bead in the fringe pattern in step 8 with a 4mm faceted glass bead. About 1 in. (2.5cm) from the centerpiece, replace the 4mm faceted glass bead with a 6mm faceted glass bead.

[10] After you add a fringe through the last bead before the centerpiece, sew through the beadwork, tying half-hitches between beads to secure the thread ends. Glue the knots and trim the thread.

[11] Repeat steps 4–10 for the necklace's other half.

[12] String a crimp on each end. String one end through the loop on half the clasp and back through the crimp and a few beads. Tighten the wire and crimp the crimp bead (Basics). Repeat at the other end.

MATERIALS
- 30mm grapevine bead (from project on p. 31-32)
- **2** 12mm pressed-glass leaf beads, top-drilled
- **14** 10mm teardrop glass beads, purple
- 8mm faceted glass bead
- **2** 2 x 4mm glass rondelles
- **2** gold-tone spacer beads
- size 6º seed beads, 10g each of the following colors: lavender and lilac
- size 11º seed beads, 25g each of the following colors: purple and green
- magatamas or size 8º seed beads, 10g green iris
- **24–30** 4mm Czech fire-polished crystals, iridescent purple
- **10–12** 6mm Czech fire-polished crystals, purple
- clasp
- **2** crimp beads
- 30 in. (76cm) flexible beading wire, .014
- Nymo thread

TOOLS & SUPPLIES
- crimping pliers
- diagonal wire cutters
- alligator clips or hemostats

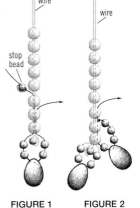

FIGURE 1   **FIGURE 2**

FIGURE 3

BEADS

Filigree finery

Create delicate, lacy beads made of polymer clay

by **Aya Teshima**

Filigree beads impart a sense of style to any creation they grace. You can take this elegant openwork a step further by adding a small charm or bell to the inside for a special touch. Embellish your bead with a dusting of metallic powder for a colorful luster.

Make the base structure

[1] To make a hollow version of this bead, skip to step 2. To insert an object, make a lengthwise slit slightly longer than the object near the end of a cornstarch packing peanut. Move your knife back and forth in the peanut to create a cavity, keeping the opening as small as possible. Insert the object (**photo a**) and squeeze the opening shut.

[2] Trim the piece of foam into a round shape about ⁵⁄₁₆ in. (8mm) in diameter, or as desired. If you inserted an object, make sure it is not exposed.

[3] Cut the polymer clay into quarters, then cut one of the quarters into thirds (**photo b**). Each of these pieces makes one bead. Condition one piece to make your first bead (see Basics, p. 5);

condition the other pieces as needed.

[4] Roll the piece of clay into a log. Then keep rolling until you create a rope that is ¹⁄₁₆ in. (2mm) in diameter. Cut the rope into five pieces, each approximately 6 in. (15cm) long (**photo c**).

[5] Place the trimmed packing peanut on one of the clay ropes, wrap the rope around the foam, and let the ends overlap slightly (**photo d**). Cut one rope to that size. Cut two more pieces of rope about ⅛ in. (3mm) longer than the first.

[6] Wrap the short piece cut in step 5 around the foam, positioning it alongside the slit (**photo e**). Press the ends together and smooth them with a needle tool. Crooked or uneven ropes make a more interesting bead, but neat seams make it easier to decorate the bead later.

[7] Wrap a second rope around the foam so it intersects the first, dividing the foam into four sections. Repeat with the third rope, forming eight sections. This becomes the base structure of the bead. Let the clay rest if it gets sticky.

Embellish the bead

Place the bead on a small piece of parchment paper so you can rotate it easily when adding decorative elements.

[1] Use the remaining clay ropes to form vines. To vary the size, roll portions of the ropes so they're thick in some places and thin in others.

[2] Press one end of a rope against the base structure and wrap it around in curving lines. Press the rope gently against the base to attach it. Smooth the end seams (**photo f**).

[3] Fill in any wide gaps with short vines.

[4] Cut the remaining pieces of rope into ³⁄₁₆-in. (5mm) slices and roll the pieces into balls. Don't try to make the balls uniform in size.

[5] To make leaves, flatten a ball into a thin oval. Use the needle tool or other pointed tool to add a center vein. Pinch the ends into points. Place each leaf on the base structure using the needle tool. Position each leaf so its ends touch the vines (**photo g**). Point the leaves in different directions so they appear randomly placed. Use leaves to span

a

b

open areas and to cover seams.

[6] To make flowers, flatten a ball into a circle on the tip of your finger. Use a pointed tool to cut an X in the top of the clay, then make a second X between the lines of the first one. Continue the cuts along the edge to create the look of petals. Place each flower on the base as desired, covering any exposed seams (**photo h**).

[7] To make dots, cut a ball into thirds and roll the pieces into smaller balls. Place the dots wherever the base structure looks bare (**photo i**). Flatten them with a needle tool or your fingernail.

Finish the bead

[1] Brush Pearl Ex Pigment Powders on the clay as follows: green pearl for leaves, interference violet for flowers and leaf accents, copper for dots, and antique gold for vines and bare spots. Apply the powders unevenly to get an antique look (**photo j**).

[2] Bake the bead at 275°F (135°C) for 45 minutes. Let the bead cool, then hold it under running water to melt the foam. Let the bead dry completely. (The beads do not get completely hard after baking and should be slightly springy.)

[3] Put the bead on a wood skewer and coat the surface with a water-based finish such as Flecto's Varathane Diamond Wood Finish. Let the first coat dry before applying a second one.

MATERIALS
- 2-oz. pkg. Premo clay, black
- Pearl Ex powders: antique gold, green pearl, copper, interference violet
- cornstarch foam pieces (magicnudles.com)
- ⁵⁄₁₆ in. (8mm) or smaller bell or charm (optional)
- Varathane Diamond Wood Finish, water-based
- parchment paper

TOOLS & SUPPLIES
- small paintbrush
- needle tool
- plastic modeling tool kit (optional)
- pasta machine*
- toaster or convection oven*

*Dedicated to nonfood use

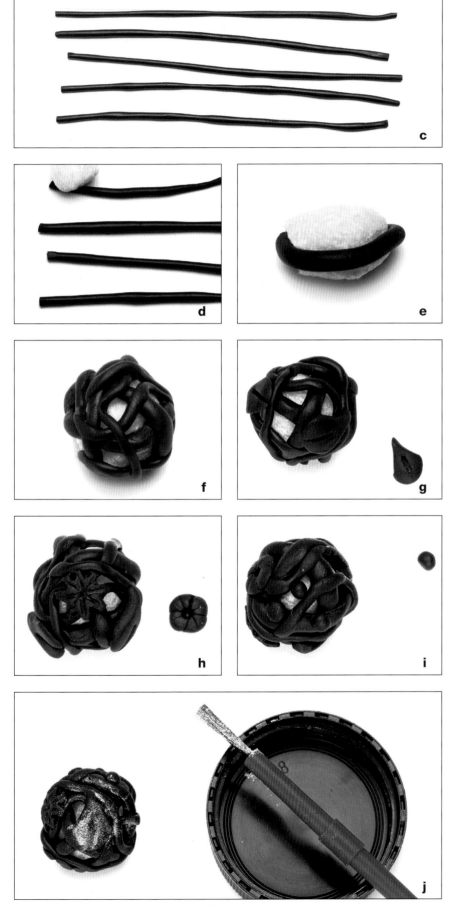

Go fish

Make a splash with polymer clay and gemstones

by **Christi Friesen**

Meet Harold. He's a flamboyant fish with a happy-go-lucky grin and an inquisitive stare. At 3 in. (7.6cm) long, this focal bead is a keeper! To create your own "fishy pet," mold a polymer-clay body and embellish it with clay accents, pearls, and gemstones. Wire in all the beads, even if there are hundreds, because your finished focal bead must be durable as well as fabulous. How sad would it be to have an eyeless fish?

Prepare the clay

[1] Condition the clay (see Basics, p. 5).
[2] Mix the body color by combining 2 oz. (56g) of sap green with Hershey Kiss-sized chunks of both ecru and gold. Run the clay through a pasta machine until thoroughly blended.
[3] Make two new hues – green accent and gold accent colors – by adjusting the balance used for the body color.
[4] You will also use gold clay straight from the package and gold clay crackled with foil. To add foil to the clay, run a little gold clay through a pasta machine so it is 1/16 in. (2mm) thick. Lay the clay sheet on white paper, then place a sheet of gold foil on top of the clay. Gently pick up the clay with the foil and run them through the pasta machine until about 1/32 in. (1mm) thick.

[5] View the four colors of clay together and adjust blends if needed (**photo a**).

Build the body

[1] Roll and manipulate the green body clay into a fish shape (**photo b**). Place it on clean, white cardstock.
[2] Smooth all sides. Pinch the tips of the tail into flattened points. Then adjust the mouth until you are pleased with his expression. (Or is your fish a *her*?)
[3] When satisfied with the overall look, make a stringing hole. Push a needle tool through the top of the head, then insert the 16-gauge wire (**photo b**).

Add accents

[1] Carve out the eye socket using a clay sculpting tool. Roll a little gold accent clay into a ball. Place it in the

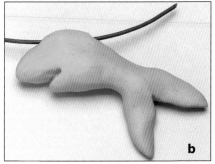

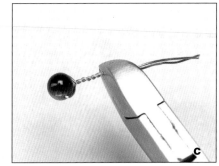

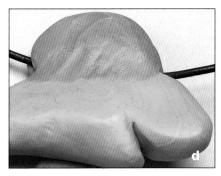

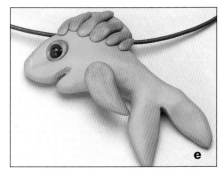

socket and flatten the ball with your finger. Smooth the edges. Check your fish's expression; since much of his personality relies on it, you'll want to make it as engaging as possible. Set your fish aside.

[2] Select a solid-color tiger-eye bead that is darker than the rest of the fish. The eye makes the piece, so choose wisely. Center a 4mm tiger-eye bead on a 2-in. (5cm) length of 28-gauge wire. Twist the wire ends together using pliers. Continue until the wire twists firmly against the bead. Trim the end with wire cutters, leaving a ¼-in. (6mm) tail (**photo c**). Push the wired bead, wire first, into the clay ball and socket. (**Photo e** shows the eye properly set.)

[3] Turn your fish over on the paper to start making the top fin panel. Roll green accent clay into a flat semicircle. Attach it to the back of the head, blending to create a firm connection (**photo d**).

[4] Turn the fish over. For the top fin, roll green accent clay into thin cylinders; flatten and press them to attach to the fin (**photo e**). Next, work on the bottom fin by rolling green accent clay into a teardrop shape. Flatten and press it onto the body securely (**photo e**).

MATERIALS
- **2** 2-oz. (56g) pkgs. Premo Sculpey, sap green
- **2** 2-oz. (56g) pkgs. Premo Sculpey, ecru
- 2-oz. (56g) pkg. Premo Sculpey, gold
- gold leaf*
- 4 in. (10cm) 16-gauge wire
- 4mm round tiger-eye bead
- 24 in. (61cm) 28-gauge wire
- **5–8** rough emerald, malachite, peridot, turquoise, or apatite gemstones
- **10** rice-shaped freshwater pearls, green tinted
- acrylic paint: burnt umber and burnt sienna
- Sculpey Glaze Satin or other clear varnish

TOOLS & SUPPLIES
- pasta machine**
- toaster or convection oven**
- craft knife or tissue blade
- cardstock or index cards
- needle tool
- clay sculpting tool
- flatnose pliers
- wire cutters
- needlenose pliers (optional)
- crochet hook or skewer
- paintbrush
- sponge
- baking sheet

*Use Magic Leaf, sold through craft stores and online, or Monarch's 23K gold leaf from misterart.com

**Dedicated to nonfood use

[5] Make smaller strips with the gold accent and the foiled clay; flatten the strips and press them between the bigger fin strips. Similarly, add thin strips of both accent colors to the tail, bottom fin, and mouth, curling the strips as desired (**photo f**).

[6] Next to the eye, add crescent shapes of green accent clay, gold accent clay, then foiled gold clay. Press the three additions gently but securely into place (**photo f**).

Embellish the fish

[1] Use all the colors, individually or combined, to make little strips of clay (**photo g**) and place them as desired. Alternate color placement to add contrast. Press and blend the fin strips where they meet the body. Repeat with the tail strips.

[2] Cut tiny rectangles of foiled gold clay. Attach them to your fish, using the tip of your craft knife to pick up and place them. Cut a pinwheel swirl out of

g

h

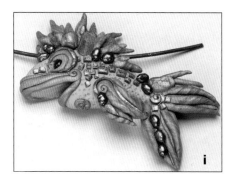

i

j

k

[5] Pick up your fish and the cardstock, place both on the baking sheet, and bake according to the manufacturer's directions. (This fish was baked at 275°F/135°C for 30 minutes.) Let the piece cool. When it is warm but able to be held comfortably, remove the 16-gauge wire from the stringing hole, gently twisting and pulling with pliers. Let your fish cool completely.

Finish the fish
[1] Add a patina to the entire top of the fish by painting it with a mixture of burnt umber and burnt sienna acrylics (**photo k**). Paint a quarter section, then wipe off the paint with a slightly damp sponge. Only the clay's crevices should retain the paint, so work quickly and carefully. If painting makes you uncomfortable, practice on spare clay or omit this step entirely.
[2] Coat the clay – whether you opted for the patina or not – with a clear, protective glaze. Place your fish on fresh cardstock on a tray and place in the oven. Bake at 200°F (93°C) for 10 minutes to set the glaze. Remove and cool.

[3] Your focal bead is done. All you have left is to name your fish. Harold would be honored if you name your masterpiece after him.

the foiled clay and place it at the tail's base. Add three foiled squares behind the swirl (**photo h**).
[3] String gemstones and pearls on wire as in step 2 of the previous section. Push the beads into the clay to accent the body (**photo i**). Use needlenose pliers to place beads in the tight spots. If the wires aren't completely hidden, add a little clay on top as camouflage.
[4] When you are satisfied with the embellishments, dimple the body for texture, using a crochet hook or skewer. Then sign your name or your initials with the needle tool on a small disk of gold clay; attach the label to the belly (**photo j**) or in some other inconspicuous spot.

CANES AND CHAINS

Canes are a foundation of polymer-clay design. Whether simple or complex, canes enable you to create fabulous patterns and color combinations out of the most basic material.

Form clay into ropes, form the ropes into rings, and form the rings into chains – you'll see that polymer clay can be the framework for your design as easily as it can be the focus.

Complex canework

Make exquisite polymer clay canes featuring chrysanthemums

by **Sarajane Helm**

In ancient Asia, chrysanthemums were grown for food and medicine, but the Chinese began growing them for beauty as early as the 5th century A.D., when a renowned official resigned his post to raise mums in pots. A century later, chrysanthemums were introduced to the Japanese, who applied many of the cultivation techniques they used with bonsai. Before long, the chrysanthemum was so popular that the Japanese Imperial Family – a hereditary monarchy that traces its lineage back to the 6th century B.C. – adopted it as its royal crest. The chrysanthemum is a central motif in Japanese culture, particularly in textiles and art, and this "Emperor of Flowers" translates beautifully to complex canework.

The secret to creating fabulous detail in a cane is to start out large. Only by making enough cane will you be able to manipulate it to form complex patterns such as these chrysanthemum designs.

Start by blending colors and making snakes. Wrap the snakes with highlight colors and combine them into larger canes. Reduce and combine them again until you've created the elaborate canes shown here.

Prepare the clay

The petals in these flowers range from dark at the center to light at the outside, with white on the edge of the outermost petals. A touch of gold at the center adds sparkle, and each petal is outlined in black.

Mix three shades of red and three shades of green in dark, medium, and light tones. Don't make the shades too subtle; the tones should be distinguishable from each other (**photo a**).

[1] Form a snake about ¾ in. (1.9cm) in diameter and 12 to 18 in. long (30–46cm) with half the dark red clay.
[2] For medium red, add enough white clay to the remaining red to produce a good medium tint and roll it into a snake twice as long as the first one.
[3] Cut 1 in. (2.5cm) of clay off each end of the medium red snake and mix it with enough white to create a much lighter tint. This snake needs to be twice as long as the medium red one. Repeat steps 1–3 with the green clay.

Make leaf canes

[1] Using a pasta machine at a medium setting, make a long sheet of white clay wide enough to wrap around three-fourths of the light red snake's circumference, leaving red exposed at the bottom. Smooth the pieces together, making sure no air bubbles are trapped between layers (**photo b**).
[2] Reduce the diameter of this snake until it is the same as the other two.
[3] With the pasta machine at a thinner setting than in step 1, make a thin sheet of black clay wide enough to cover about three-fourths of each snake's circumference, as in step 1 of this section. Wrap all three snakes in a layer of black, again leaving the bottom uncovered. Don't worry about

slight imperfections (**photo c**).
[4] Roll the light green clay into a snake about the diameter of your thumb. Cut lengthwise through the snake to make two half-circles.
[5] With the pasta machine at the same setting as step 1, make long sheets of dark and medium green clay. To make the vein, cut the dark green sheet into a 1-in.-wide (2.5cm) strip as long as the light green snake and sandwich it between the two half-circles of light green.
[6] Trim away the excess. Use the medium green sheet to wrap the leaf cane completely (**photo d**).

Make chrysanthemum canes

[1] Lightly pinch the bottoms of the dark, medium, and light red snakes to create a teardrop (or petal) shape, with the bottom of the teardrop displaying the petal color.
[2] Cut the dark red snake into six equal lengths about 2 to 3 in. (5–7.6cm) each. Use one of these as a guide for cutting the medium red snake. Cut as many pieces of equal length as you can, reducing the snake slightly to increase its length if necessary.
[3] Cut the light red snake in half, set one half aside, and cut the other into pieces as in step 2.
[4] Roll a ⅜-in. (1cm) snake of gold clay for the center. Cut the gold snake

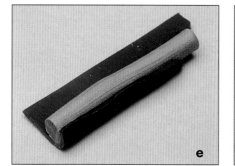

e

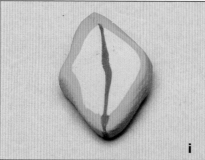

f

g

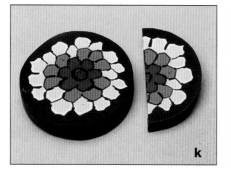

h

i

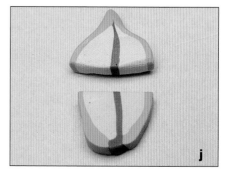

j

k

l

m

to the same length and wrap with a thin sheet of black clay (**photo e**).

[5] To begin assembling the flower, place the dark red pieces around the gold with the pointed ends touching the center and the rounded ends outward. This will use up your dark red snake.

[6] Surround the first layer with medium red pieces, setting the pointed ends into the grooves. Skip one or two grooves as needed to go around the

entire circumference evenly. Repeat with the light red pieces.

[7] Working with the reserved portion of the light red snake, use your thumb and forefinger to flatten the point at the bottom and pinch the point and top of the petal along the snake's length to widen the cane. These outermost petals should be broader than the others. Build the fourth layer of petals with these pieces. (You can add more layers and more gradations of colors if you wish.) Fill the remaining grooves with triangle-shaped black pieces (**photo f**).

[8] Gently squeeze the entire cane along its length to compress the pieces and remove any air. Check the cane's top and bottom faces to make sure they are aligned and the petals are where you want them.

[9] Use the pasta machine at the thinnest setting to make a thin sheet of black clay, then wrap the entire cane.

(Do this twice if you have enough clay. The extra layer protects the image from distortion during reduction.) Roll the entire cane gently to make sure the wrap is smooth with no air pockets (**photo g**). Let the cane rest for at least an hour before you reduce it. This allows the outer portions to cool, so the inside and outside will reduce more evenly, and it helps the component pieces of the cane adhere to each other.

[10] Reduce the cane to about 1 in. (2.5cm) in diameter by a combination of rolling and squeezing. Remember that the secret to complex canes is to start out with large canes; these canes may start as wide as soft-drink cans before they can be carefully reduced to a 1-in. (2.5cm) or smaller diameter (**photo h**).

[11] After reduction, cut off the first 1–2 in. (2.5–5cm) on each end until you come to the clear image. Set these scraps aside for another project.

MATERIALS

- Fimo Soft or Premo Sculpey, one 2-oz. (56g) pkg. each of the following colors: cadmium red, green, and gold
- ¾ lb. (340g) any polymer clay, white
- 1 lb. (454g) any polymer clay, black

TOOLS & SUPPLIES

- pasta machine*
- toaster or convection oven*
- brayer or acrylic rod
- tissue blade or NuBlade
- plastic wrap

*Dedicated to nonfood use

Make leaves

[1] Reduce the leaf cane to the diameter of the finished flower or smaller and pinch the top and bottom at the vein to form a leaf shape (photo i).

[2] Cut the cane into 3- to 4-in. (7.6–10cm) sections, reducing its diameter if necessary to get pieces of equal length. Working at a right angle to the vein, slice one of the sections lengthwise (photo j). Stand the section on end to make the cutting easier.

Assemble the complex cane

[1] Cut two 3-in. (7.6cm) lengths of the flower cane. Wrap the rest of the cane in plastic wrap to keep it from drying out.

[2] Reduce one of the flower canes to a ¾-in. (1.9cm) diameter and trim it to 3 in. Cut in half lengthwise to create two half-flower sections. Place one alongside the uncut flower cane (photo k).

[3] Gently shape the other half-flower section into a circle and place it alongside the other two flower canes.

[4] Place the whole leaf and half-leaf sections around the flower cluster and fill in the spaces with triangular black pieces to round out the cane as in step 7 of the "Make Chrysanthemum Canes" section above (photo l). Try not to have any leaf or flower color showing on the outside of the cane.

Variations on a complex cane

Canes can be as simple or as complex as you desire. The trick is to look at a design you want to duplicate and then break it down color by color, part by part. But what if you want to take that design a step further? Simply rearranging elements can give you a whole new look. Here are some suggestions to vary the chrysanthemum complex cane you just made.

[1] For a square repeat pattern, start with two equal sections of complex cane. Slice one section in half lengthwise into half-circles, then cut each of these in half again so you have four quartered sections (photo a).

[2] Place each quarter around the uncut cane with its right-angle corner facing outward. These become the corners of the square cane. Fill in the open spaces with small pieces of black clay or some other background color (photo b).

[3] Squeeze the square cane to compress it. Using even pressure, reduce it by working up and down its length on all four sides equally with your hands or a brayer or an acrylic rod.

[4] For a patchwork effect, build a block with several square canes from step 3 (photo c). Create additional patterns by cutting and recombining the complex canes in different ways.

[5] To make striped or feathered beads, chop up the leftover bits of cane and roll them into a snake. Twist the snake to create a striped effect, then drag a stick or needle along the length to swirl the colors (photo d).

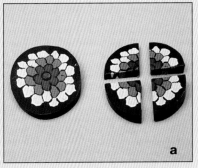

a

b

c

d

CANES AND CHAINS

[5] Gently press the cane together and reduce it to a finished diameter of 1 in. (2.5cm) or less (photo m).

[6] Form beads with your complex cane or cut slices from it. Pierce the beads and bake them according to the manufacturer's directions.

Great canes

Simple cut-and-paste techniques
expand polymer clay's possibilities

by **Lee Radtke and Sarah Shriver**

The beads shown in this project and in the green and blue necklaces are by Lee and began with a single cane design. Beads by Sarah are used in the red necklace (far left, p. 44). Even the simplest cane design will produce a multitude of complex variations when you use a computer drawing program and some easy cut-and-paste techniques. The scintillating kaleidoscopic effect shown here is a matter of design and color exploration – the more you stretch your horizons, the greater will become your mastery of these techniques.

A computer drawing program (*Painter 6* was used here) makes these color and design exercises easy and enlightening. However, you can employ the same techniques using colored pencils, along with some significant time and money spent in a copy shop. A computer drawing pad is helpful for drawing curved lines with accuracy, but if you have experience you can accomplish this with a mouse.

Keep in mind when doing these exercises that everyone starts as a beginner and improves with practice and more practice. Evaluate your steps and ask yourself frequently, "What else might I have done?" Consider that different brands of clays have different properties that affect the success of a design. Take notes and save slices of canes to document how you produced certain designs. Most of all, take joy in the "play" of these techniques and the process of exploring new possibilities. You will find the journey as satisfying as the end result.

Make the design

[1] Draw a bold pattern in black and white with straight lines and curves, crossing some shapes to get over-and-under effects (**figure 1**). Leave some shapes unfinished along the edges. Eliminate dark boundaries on the borders of your design. Open shapes will combine to make new shapes when you rejoin the patterns in sets of two or more. Keep in mind that your pattern will be compressed when you reduce your complex canes, so don't make any element too small – think bold and large for this step. If you are working on a computer, enlarge the image and mend any breaks in the lines so you can control where the colors go. Make your design's dimensions a 2-in. (5cm) square to facilitate the cutting and regrouping you will do when you design your cane patterns.

[2] After you are satisfied with your black-and-white cane design (**figure 1**), flip the design on the vertical axis to make a mirror image. Save both images and make multiple copies to color. This will be useful when you want to try other color combinations.

[3] Color one set of mirror-image copies identically (**figure 2**). Choose your colors carefully. Look for strong contrasts and avoid subtle colors to prevent muddiness when you combine and reduce your canes. Consult a color wheel or color

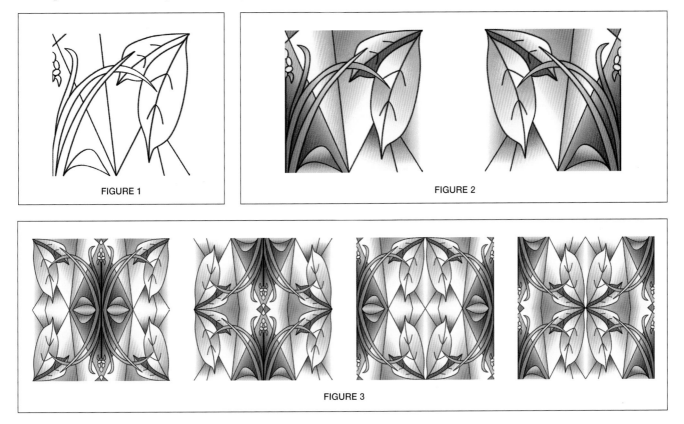

FIGURE 1

FIGURE 2

FIGURE 3

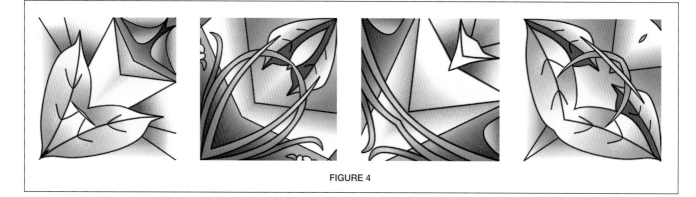

FIGURE 4

theory books if you want more guidance.
[4] Use color gradations in your design.
On a computer drawing program, they
are often called "gradients." They can
range from a dark shade to a very light
tint of the same color or a dark shade
of one color to a light tint of another.
Go for dramatic changes so the
differentiation will be apparent in the
canes you make. Notice how some tints
go almost white. These will provide
highlights in your recombined canes.
Polymer-clay color gradations are
accomplished with Skinner blends (see
Basics, p. 5). Vary the direction of the
gradations in your design – top to
bottom, side to side, bottom to top.
Keep a few areas of solid color to help
the eye focus more easily.
[5] Scrutinize your colored pattern. If
you are dissatisfied, stop and make
changes now. Careful preparation at this
stage will produce more successful canes.
[6] Save these colored mirror images.
They will be the building blocks for
more complex designs. It's easy to

duplicate the images on the computer.
If you are making your copies at a
copy shop, ask how you can make
multiple copies at the lowest price. Or
find a friend with a scanner and offer
to exchange some of the finished canes
for a little scanning. You must have an
equal number of each image in order
to combine your patterns. Make as
many copies as possible for cutting and
pasting.
[7] Explore the possible combinations
for your design. Observe how the
uncut design can be combined in
blocks of four, simply by rearranging
which sides abut together (figure 3).
Or you can cut the design diagonally
and mirror the two sections (figure 4).
Once satisfied with the design, mirror-
image cane slices were cut diagonally
and recombined to create real versions
(photo a).

Make the cane

[1] Create your design in polymer clay.
If it turns out that your design is too

difficult to duplicate in clay, don't
despair. You can eliminate parts of
your design to make it workable. If
you're set on a complex, detailed
design, use Fimo brands of clay; the
higher density of Fimo makes
complicated designs attainable. Make
your canes large-scale, perhaps 4 in.
(10cm) square. Reduce carefully,
keeping all sides even and the lines
straight. When you are combining
canes or parts of canes, carefully align
colors and lines within the design. You
may need to stretch or warp parts
slightly to make them fit.
[2] To achieve the maximum
possibilities with your cane, reduce only
one end of it, leaving the other end to
use for the ideas that will inevitably
occur to you during the process.
Explore the possibilities of cutting and
recombining composite canes or adding
new elements from the same color
spectrum. Once you get started, it will
be hard to stop (photo b).

a

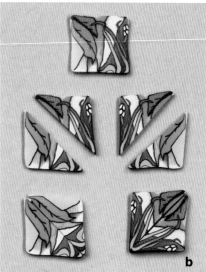

b

Loop-in-loop

Borrow a technique from wireworkers to make a chain with polymer-clay links

by **Nan Roche**

The chameleon-like charms of polymer clay are such that it may be fashioned to look like just about any jewelry medium and technique. For example, complex canes easily take on the appearance of glass *millefiori*, while clay sheet can be carved to look like wood *inro* or ivory scrimshaw; polymer clay can even mimic lacquer, porcelain, or enamel. Is it no wonder, then, that this versatile material might also be used to imitate a classic wirework technique? Chain mail, the art of using metal jump rings to weave chains of various patterns, may seem an unlikely inspiration, but the classic loop-in-loop technique translates amazingly well to polymer clay.

Just as with the traditional metal-worked version, much of the tedious part of this project is making the rings. However, modifying a clay gun for heavy-duty use makes this part of the process faster and smoother; see "Adapt a Clay Gun," p. 50, for details.

Make clay cords

[1] Roll polymer clay into a log, cut it into quarters, and stack, maintaining the same direction. Roll again. Repeat

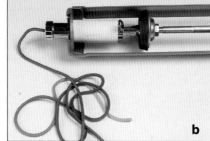

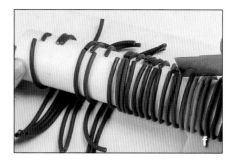

8–10 more times. This aligns the clay molecules and helps to improve the strength of the extruded cords.

[2] *Mokume gane* effects show up whenever clay layers are involved. If clay is layered before loaded into the clay gun, it will extrude with one color wrapping another. There is more resistance between the wall of the clay gun and the outside of the clay, so the clay's center flows through faster, becoming wrapped by the edge clay. To achieve these layers, roll logs of clay the diameter of the clay-gun barrel in two or more colors. Slice off ¼-in. (6mm) discs of each color and stack them alternately, making a new log. Be sure that there are no air pockets and that the log is smooth (**photo a**). Put the assembled log into the clay gun.

[3] To extrude the cord, press the trigger of the caulk gun until it presses against the handle of the clay gun. The clay will come out easily (**photo b**). Continue to press the trigger with steady pressure. Extrude the cords onto pieces of tissue paper. Try to use them the same day because they become brittle over time.

[4] There are three basic kinds of chains: simple, open, and double loop-in-loop. To form the loops, wrap the clay cords around a pipe. Experiment with different diameter cords and different diameter pipes for each of the techniques (**photo c**). If the loops are too small or large or the diameter of

the clay cords is too small or large, you'll have difficulty making the more complex loop-in-loop chains.

Simple loop-in-loop chain

Begin with a simple loop-in-loop structure, which is the basis for all the other chains.

[1] Use a ⅛-in.-diameter (3mm) disk to make the cord and wrap it around a 1½-in.-diameter (3.8cm) PVC pipe. Extrude at least two barrelsful of clay.

[2] Join two or more lengths of cord together by blunt-cutting the ends, placing them together, and gently rolling at the join without smashing or thinning the joined area (**photo d**). Attach one end of the cord to the PVC pipe, pressing firmly. Wrap the entire cord around the pipe without pulling or stretching (**photo e**).

[3] Gently rest the pipe with the cord on the work surface and use a tissue blade to slice through all the links (**photo f**). Keep them in order if you are interested in preserving the color shading effect created by the *mokume gane* extrusion.

[4] Pick up each link piece and join the ends by pressing together with a slight twisting motion. Lay the link on the work surface and gently roll with a finger to even out the clay and to achieve a good, strong join with no visible seams. Continue joining all the loops. If your room is warm and the clay is sticky or your hands are sticky,

dust a little cornstarch on your hands, or let the loops rest for an hour.

[5] Next, take the first link and squeeze it into a bowtie shape, touching in the middle (**photo g**). Fold the loop arms of the bowtie up into a flower shape, touching the loops at the tips (**photo h**). Squeeze the next link into a bowtie. Thread it through the loop arms of the first bowtie (**photo i**). Fold the second loop up into a flower shape and touch the loop arms together (**photo j**). Continue in this manner, threading loops through loops until the chain is the desired length. Be careful not to handle the growing chain too much or twist it while assembling. The unbaked clay will stick to itself with too much handling.

[6] If desired, pinch the final ends together to form a thickened area that you can drill after baking. Lay the chain on the baking surface, gently loosen all the links, and re-shape them if they have been flattened or twisted. Bake according to the manufacturer's directions. Allow the chain to cool to room temperature. When cool, areas of the chain may have fused together. Gently pull them apart and loosen the chain. You can sand and polish the chain, but polish by hand as buffing with a buffing wheel tends to be very difficult with pieces this delicate. See "Buffing Tips," (p. 82) for details.

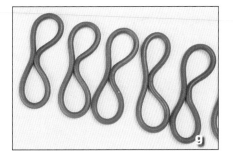

Open loop-in-loop chains

[1] Open loop-in-loop chaining follows steps 1–4 from the section on "Simple loop-in-loop chains" above. Create the links and pinch them into bowties. This time, instead of folding the end loops up, keep the bowtie flat and curve it into a U- or heart shape (**photo k**).

[2] To create the second chain from the bottom (p. 47) gently thread the next bowtie loop through the two arms of the first loop (**photo l**) and join it into a flat U again (**photo m**). Carefully weave the bowtie loops down and up through the U shapes just as if you were sewing. Continue in this manner until you have reached the desired length.

[3] If desired, pinch the final ends together to form a thickened area that you can drill. Arrange the chain on the baking surface and gently loosen all the links, shaping them as you go. Curve it in the position that you'll be wearing it. If it will be a necklace, press on the links and shape them slightly to conform to the shape of your neck. Bake the chain in this arrangement; it will lie on your neck in the same position as shaped.

[4] After baking and cooling, gently pop apart any links that are stuck together. Sand and polish to finish.

Double loop-in-loop chains

[1] Start out as for the simple loop-in-loop chain for the first two loops. Next, thread the third loop through the first loop (**photo n**). Create the space for the loop by pressing the first and second loops together to produce an opening through both loops. You might need to open the space with a pencil. Squeeze one end of the third bowtie a little tighter in order to thread it through the smaller space. It is often helpful to dust the links with cornstarch and to wiggle

MATERIALS
- Premo Sculpey clay, **2** or more colors
- rubber cord for finishing

TOOLS & SUPPLIES
- pasta machine*
- toaster or convection oven*
- tissue slicing blade
- modified clay/caulk gun (see "Adapt a Clay Gun," p. 50)
- PVC pipe, 6 x 1½-in. diameter (15 x 3.8cm)
- wet/dry sandpaper in 220-, 320-, 400-, and 600-grit
- sponge
- shallow plastic basin
- tissue or parchment paper
- drill and bit same size as rubber cord
- cyanoacrylate glue

*Dedicated to nonfood use

the link gently to get it through. The biggest problem is a tendency to pinch the clay too much as you try to thread it through, which deforms the whole chain. Continue adding loops in this manner until you have reached the desired length. Handle the growing chain with fingertips only and don't crush it.

[2] Lay out the chain on the baking surface and loosen all the links. Don't worry if some are stuck. It is better to leave them a little stuck until after baking than to over-manipulate the chain and cause them to squeeze together even more. If desired, pinch the ends together to make a solid ending that you can drill.

[3] After baking, allow the chain to cool before gently popping the links apart. This chain, shown at bottom (p. 47), is very beautiful when sanded and polished, especially if you use the layered *mokume gane* blend for the cords.

Finish the necklaces

[1] After baking, sand with wet/dry sandpaper starting with 220-grit, then 320-, 400-, and finally 600-grit (**photo o**). If you want a high shine, very carefully use a buffing machine with a muslin polishing wheel.

[2] To create a perfect toggle, use a Hornberger Bead Roller tool (**photo p**) and rubber cording that is soft and durable. (The photo shows a round

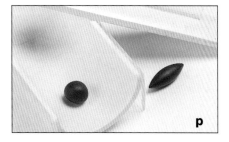

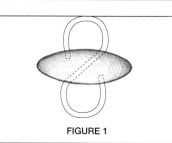

FIGURE 1

ball of clay in the trough; the paddle is pushed back and forth over the round ball, and a double-pointed oval bead, at right in the photo, emerges.) Make two toggle beads for each necklace.

[3] Use a drill fitted with a bit that is the same diameter as the cord and drill two parallel holes halfway through the first bead. On the second bead, drill a diagonal hole through the middle and a half-drilled hole on each side of it (**figure 1**).

[4] Cut two cords to the desired length. Fold one in half, place the fold through the last link on one end of the necklace, and bring both ends through the fold as shown in the open loop-in-loop necklace, second from the bottom (p. 47). String the bead with two holes. Place glue in the two parallel half-drilled holes and put the ends of the cord into them. Let dry.

[5] Apply glue to one half-drilled hole on the second bead. Place one end of the second cord through the end of the chain and into the hole with the glue. Bring the other end through the diagonal hole. Apply a small amount of glue to the second half-drilled hole and put this cord end in it as shown in the double loop-on-loop necklace, shown at the top far left (p. 47). Let set. On each end of the necklace, glue the loops of the end link together (**photo q**).

Adapt a clay gun

Clay guns consist of a barrel, a plunger, and a set of disks with holes of different shapes and sizes. Unfortunately, polymer clay is very stiff and difficult to extrude through a clay gun. To help extrude the polymer clay, make a hybrid tool using a clay gun and a caulk gun – a tool carpenters use to seal gaps, apply adhesives, and so on. The caulk gun pushes the plunger of the clay gun, which provides the extra leverage needed to make the job easy. You'll need a number of parts (**photo a**), but all are relatively inexpensive and available from any hardware store or home-improvement center.

[1] Referring to the photo (**photo a**), fit the furniture caster over the plunger part of the caulk gun. Glue it in place. This cushions the plunger handle of the clay gun and holds it in place while the caulk gun plunger pushes against it.

[2] Remove the screw cap from the clay gun's end. Slide the O-ring on the barrel and then the piece of PVC pipe so it's caught firmly on the barrel by the O-ring. Hold the pipe on the clay gun. Slip the metal washer over the barrel, add an extruding disk, and replace the screw cap of the clay gun.

[3] To use, simply add polymer clay to the canister of the clay gun and begin squeezing the trigger of the caulk gun. The caulk gun's mechanism will press against the clay, and the pressure will force the clay to begin extruding. Periodically press the caulk gun's trigger to maintain even pressure.

MATERIALS

- clay gun (available from art or polymer-clay supply stores)
- COX caulk gun (the ratchet action of this brand requires little force to operate)
- PVC pipe, 2 x 1-in. (5 x 2.5cm) diameter
- rubber O-ring, ⅞-in. (2.2cm) diameter
- metal washer, 2-in.-outside diameter with a ⅞-in.-diameter hole
- ½-in. (1.3cm) round rubber furniture caster

Chains of clay

Link polymer clay split rings to create jewelry

by **Vicki J. Wulwick**

Is it possible to make durable split rings with polymer clay? You might not think so, but polymer clay is up to the challenge. Using primarily the ⅛-in. (3mm) round opening on a clay extruder (or, in the case of the bottom right necklace, p. 51, the quatrefoil opening), long strands of extruded clay can be wrapped around almost anything to achieve the right size link for a project. For example, a pair of size 9 knitting needles was used for the black and gold necklace's links. Both ½-in. (1.3cm) and ⅜-in. (1cm) wood dowels were used for the bracelets' links. These are only a fraction of the size links you can make. Don't limit this technique to only jewelry, either – you can make everything from belts to napkin rings to more, so feel free to experiment!

Make and connect split rings

[1] Condition the clay (see Basics, p. 5).
[2] Roll a cylinder of clay about ½ in. (1.3cm) in diameter and 3 in. (7.6cm) long. Put it in the extruder with a ⅛-in. round opening and extrude a snake. Avoid distorting the snake as it extrudes (**photo a**).

[3] Wrap the snake around the wood dowel or other cylindrical tool, keeping the wraps snug and even along its length (**photo b**). You will need 40–50 full rotations to make a bracelet and at least 120–140 full rotations for a neckline-length necklace. Make a few extra wraps for attaching dangles.
[4] Bake the coils on the dowels at 295°F (146°C) for 30 minutes. (*Editor's Note:* Dowel rods usually come in 3 ft./.9m lengths, so make sure to cut them to fit your oven *before* wrapping on the extruded clay.)
[5] When the pieces have cooled, use a craft knife to slice the wrapped clay at regular two-wrap intervals (**photo c**), or basically every other loop. Make a clasp by cutting one split ring with three wraps or use a two-wrap split ring made on a slightly larger-circumference dowel.
[6] To assemble a chain, link the two-wrap split rings together by wrapping one through the coils of another (**photo d**). You may need to loosen the coils with your fingernail. Check the chain length against your wrist or neck as you assemble it and adjust accordingly.
[7] Although the rings are surprisingly strong, you can secure them with a dot of cyanoacrylate glue at the ends of each ring – a step that's recommended when making an especially long chain.
[8] Connect the two ends of the necklace or bracelet chain with a three-wrap or a larger two-wrap split ring.

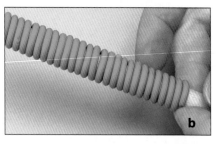

MATERIALS
- Premo Sculpey, any colors
- metallic powder (optional)

TOOLS & SUPPLIES
- pasta machine*
- toaster or convection oven*
- clay extruder with a variety of hole shapes and sizes
- wood dowels, ⅜–¾ in. (1–1.9cm), cut to fit into the oven used
- knitting needles (optional)
- craft knife
- rubber stamps (optional)
- cookie and clay cutters*
- plastic drinking straw*
- cyanoacrylate glue

*Dedicated to nonfood use

Make and attach dangles

[1] Run a clay sheet through the pasta machine on the appropriate setting. (You can use plain clay for stamping or make a more elaborate sheet using *mokune gane* or cane slices.) Use a medium-thick setting if you are going to stamp the clay and a medium setting if you're only cutting dangle shapes. You also can use cane slices for dangles.
[2] Before stamping the clay, brush some metallic powder on the stamp to highlight the image, if you like.
[3] Use a cookie or clay cutter to slice shapes. Pierce them close to the top edge with a drinking straw.
[4] Bake at 295°F (146°C) for 30 minutes. Allow the clay to cool.
[5] Insert one end of a single-wrap ring (a standard jump ring) into a dangle's hole. Apply a dot of glue on one end and glue the ends together (**photo e**).
[6] When the glue is dry, attach the dangle's ring to a split ring on the necklace or bracelet.

Explore the diversity of polymer clay with these widely different pendant projects. Each capitalizes on a unique aspect of the clay, some add new materials or found objects, and all provide a distinctive and creative focal point for your jewelry.

Primitive pendant

by **Donna Kato**

For this ethnic-style pendant, compose several canes using deep, earthy colors. When you are satisfied that they will work well together, start thinking about a shape that will best use the colors and patterns of your canes. This pendant takes the shape of a thin leaf with a definite ridge down the center and is made with three canes: a striped loaf, a feather tip, and a maze. The maze cane was made with Skinner-blend sheets and leftover canes from past projects; as such, your maze cane won't look like the one shown in this project. If you don't have any leftovers to make a maze cane, begin with only two sheets of contrasting colors. Roll the layered sheet in a random manner to create amazingly intricate designs when the cane is reduced and assembled.

Prepare the clay

[1] Condition the clay (see Basics, p. 5) until it is soft and pliable.

[2] Make three Skinner-blend sheets (Basics) in the following color combinations, using 1 oz. (28g), or half a package, of each color: Indian red to mandarin, Sahara to caramel, gold to chocolate.

[3] Roll up each Skinner-blend sheet tightly from one graded edge to the other. Do not make a shaded bull's-eye cane, rolling one color edge to the other. Rather, you should have a shaded cylinder with one color at each end (**photo a,** left).

[4] Roll each cylinder while pressing gently with your hands from the ends into the center. This process reduces the cylinder's length and increases its width. Continue until your cylinders are a stout 1½–2 in. (3.8–5cm) long and resemble a shaded hockey puck (**photo a,** right). You will slice pieces from these three compressed cylinders to construct the maze cane.

Maze cane

[1] Run black clay through the pasta machine to create a sheet ¹⁄₁₆ in. (2mm) thick. Trim the sheet into a 10 x 2-in. (25 x 5cm) rectangular strip.

[2] Cut slices from the compressed cylinders. Flatten with your fingers or roll through the pasta machine until the slices are 2 in. (5cm) wide.

[3] Arrange these new Skinner-blend slices and any leftover cane pieces from previous projects on the black sheet (**photo b**). If you don't have any leftovers, follow the suggestion from the introduction.

[4] Roll up the black sheet tightly and compress it to squeeze out air pockets (**photo c**, left). Work the cane into a triangular shape by pressing the sides of the cane against your work surface (**photo c**, center). Pinch ridges at the corners of the triangle. Flip side to side, sharpening the ridges. Reduce and lengthen the cane by gently stroking the sides as you stretch it. Be careful not to twist it. Flip the cane frequently, working all sides evenly until the cane is 12 in. (30cm) long.

[5] Slice the cane in half and press one side to the other so they mirror each other (**photo c**, right).

[6] Slice this combined cane into thirds and assemble the pieces into a hexagon (**photo d**). Roll a brayer or an acrylic rod along the six sides to sharpen the corners.

Striped-loaf cane

[1] Using 1 oz. (28g), or half a package, each of caramel and black clay, run each color through the pasta machine at the thickest setting.

[2] Layer the sheets and trim into a square or rectangle.

[3] Run the combined sheet through at the thickest setting again.

[4] Cut the sheet in half and stack one half on top of the other, making sure the colors alternate (**photo e**, left). Cut and stack two more times to make a striped loaf. Trim the sides (**photo e**, right).

Feather-tip cane

[1] Run 1 oz. (28g), or half a package, of gold clay through the pasta machine at the thickest setting. Trim with a tissue blade or NuBlade to make a square or rectangle.

[2] Cut a package of Indian red polymer clay in half and run each half through the pasta machine at the middle setting.

[3] Place the gold sheet between the red sheets and trim.

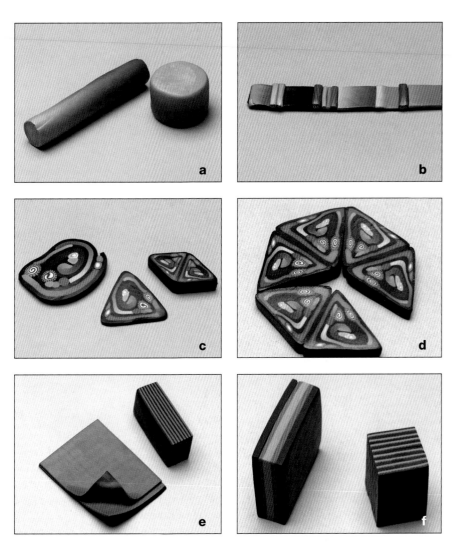

[4] Cut a package of black clay in half and run each half through the pasta machine at the thickest setting. Sandwich the red and gold stack between the black sheets (**photo f**, left).

[5] Roll out the sandwich with a brayer or an acrylic rod until it is slightly thicker than the thickest setting on the pasta machine (about ⅛ in./3mm). Run the sheet through the pasta machine on the thickest setting.

[6] Cut the sheet in half and stack the pieces. Repeat twice. Neaten the sides.

[7] Stand the cane on end. Trim so that the face of the cane is square (**photo f**, right).

[8] Slowly and carefully cut the cane in half on the diagonal (**photo g**). Turn one half over so that the stripes form a V when the two halves are put together (**photo h**), but don't abut the pieces yet.

[9] Using ½ oz. (14g), or a quarter of a

package of gold and 1 oz. (28g) each of Indian red and black, repeat steps 1–5. Insert a piece of this sheet between the two halves of the slab you made in step 8; abut together. Save the rest for later.

Construct the pendant

[1] Roll scrap clay into a cylinder 3 in. (7.6cm) long and ¾ in. (1.9cm) in diameter. Taper the ends of the cylinder.

[2] Mold the cylinder into a triangular shape with tapered ends. Flatten the back side, leaving the two front sides slightly curved. The front sides will be covered with pattern sheets made from the canes.

[3] Make a pattern sheet with each cane. Do not overlap the cane slices.

MATERIALS
- Fimo Soft, **2** 2-oz. (56g) pkgs. each of the following colors: black (#9), caramel (#7), and Indian red (#24)
- Fimo Soft, one 2-oz. (56g) pkg. each of the following colors: Sahara (#70), mandarin (#42), chocolate (#75), and gold (#11)
- leftover canes and scrap clay for maze canes, pattern sheet base, and pendant-body interior
- 30-in. (76cm) Buna cord (available from auto-supply stores or prairiecraft.com)
- small rubber gaskets (optional)

TOOLS & SUPPLIES
- pasta machine*
- toaster or convection oven*
- tissue blade or NuBlade
- brayer or acrylic rod
- needle tool or craft knife
- bamboo skewer
- wet/dry sandpaper in 400- and 600-grit (optional)
- electric buffer and buffing wheel (optional)
- Polar Fleece (optional)
- cyanoacrylate glue

*Dedicated to nonfood use

Cut and arrange them so they fit together precisely (**photo i**): Begin with a thin sheet of scrap clay. Cut thin slices from your canes and arrange them on the sheet. Roll lightly over the sheet with a brayer or an acrylic rod to smooth and join the cane seams. Run the sheet through the pasta machine at the middle setting. Note: Running striped slices horizontally through the rollers will widen them; running them vertically will elongate them.

[**4**] Cut pieces of the sheets to cover the two front sides of the pendant. For the project shown, vertical-stripe slices were placed at the top of the pendant on each side. The feather-tip sheet was used for the remainder of one side and the maze pattern on the other side. Make sure there are no air pockets between the sheets and the pendant body.

[**5**] Cut thin strips from the layered sheet made in step 9 of the feather-tip cane. Use the strips to cover the seams where the pattern sheets meet (**photo j**). If you like, roll the remainder of this sheet into a jelly roll and cut a slice to apply to the pendant, as shown on the feather-tip side of the project pendant. Smooth the sides with a brayer or an acrylic rod.

[**6**] Run a thick slice from the Sahara and chocolate cylinder through the pasta machine at the medium setting to make a sheet large enough to cover the back of the pendant.

[**7**] Place the backing sheet on a piece of paper and position the pendant on the sheet. Using the needle tool or a craft knife, trim the clay from around the pendant. Pick up the pendant and inspect the back side. Pierce and remove any air pockets. Smooth the edges.

[**8**] Pierce the pendant with the skewer to make a hole about 1 in. (2.5cm) from the top point and ¼ in. (6mm) from the back. Enter from the opposite direction to smooth the hole's exit side.

[**9**] Bake the pendant for 45 minutes in a 265°F (130°C) oven. This is a thick pendant, so if you follow a different manufacturer's directions for baking, adjust accordingly. Cool before handling.

Finish the pendant

[**1**] For a high-gloss shine, sand the piece under water with 400- and then 600-grit wet/dry sandpaper. Rub the piece with a soft cloth or paper towel to remove any residue.

[**2**] Using circular motions, buff the piece on an electric buffer to bring out a high-gloss shine. If you do not have an electric buffer, rub the pendant on a piece of Polar Fleece to bring out a satin finish.

[**3**] If you wish to apply a water-based glaze instead of following steps 1–2, sand the piece first to improve the finished appearance.

Make a necklace

Insert a Buna cord end into the bead hole until it is halfway in. If you are using gaskets, slide them onto the cord. Apply a drop of glue to the other end of the Buna cord and insert it into the opposite side of the hole until the ends touch inside. Hold until the glue grabs, then slide the gaskets over the bead holes.

Leaf pendants

Polymer clay provides the medium and nature the inspiration for this project

by **Patricia Kimle**

Begin this multistep project, a lovely necklace and earring set, by making molds of real leaves, though you also can use other natural objects such as shells or starfish. Sculpey SuperFlex Bake & Bend modeling compound was used to make the molds, but use the flexible modeling product of your choice. Make your elements with polymer clay. Finally, dust the molded polymer-clay elements with metallic powders for subtle highlights.

Make a leaf mold

[1] Condition (see Basics, p. 5) and run ½ oz. (14g) of Sculpey SuperFlex Bake & Bend modeling compound through a pasta machine on the middle setting. Cut the clay into a 3-in. (7.6cm) square, or about ½ in. (1.3cm) larger on all sides than the leaf to be molded (**photo a**).

[2] Brush the clay with cornstarch to remove tackiness. Lay the leaf on the clay and roll both through the pasta machine on the same setting as in

step 1 (**photo b**). Carefully separate the leaf from the clay.

[3] Repeat steps 1–2 to make a second mold using another leaf.

[4] Make two smaller leaf molds if you plan to make earrings.

[5] Bake the clay sheets according to the manufacturer's directions. (These were baked at 285°F/140°C for 20 minutes.) Allow the clay to cool.

Shape the base beads

[1] Form a base bead for the pendant by conditioning and rolling black polymer clay into a teardrop shape, approximately 1 x 1½ x ⅜ in. (2.5 x 3.8 x 1cm). Texture the surface with a coarse sanding sponge (**photo c**).

[2] For earrings, make and texture two teardrops approximately ¾ x 1 x ¼ in. (1.9cm x 2.5cm x 6mm) each.

[3] Pierce each base bead all the way through with a needle tool. For a pendant with a partial piercing (the right-hand pendant, p. 57), push the needle tool only halfway through the base bead

(**photo d**), then remove the tool.

[4] Bake the base beads according to the manufacturer's directions. Allow the clay to cool.

Mold the leaves

[1] Make sheets of black clay the same size and thickness as the leaf molds. Brush the sheets with cornstarch.

[2] Run a sheet of clay and a mold together through the pasta machine on its widest setting. Carefully peel apart the mold and the clay (**photo e**).

[3] With a craft knife, trim the excess clay around the leaf (**photo f**). Add a light coating of Translucent Liquid Sculpey (TLS) to the back of the leaf

(**photo g**). Gently press the leaf onto the textured base bead.

[4] Repeat steps 1–3 with the remaining molds and bases.

[5] Using your finger, dab small amounts of Pearl Ex Pigment Powder across the surface of the clay leaves (**photo h**), varying the colors of the powders; remove any color that accidentally gets on the base bead. Bake according to the manufacturer's directions, then allow to cool.

Make jewelry

[1] For a pendant bead pierced end to end, bend one end of the 19-gauge wire into a small spiral with roundnose

EDITOR'S NOTE: Pasta-machine settings vary. To determine the appropriate thickness for your leaf mold, select a setting that is just over half the thickness of your pasta machine's thickest setting. To double-check your selection, roll clay at a medium thickness and fold it in half. Run it through on your thickest setting. It should not get much longer—no more than about 10 percent of folded length. If it doesn't elongate at all, then the setting is too thin.

g

h

i

j

k

pliers. Flatten the spiral with a ballpeen hammer and anvil (**photo i**).

[2] String a 4mm bead, a polymer-clay bead pierced through the center, a spacer, and an oval bead. Make a wrapped loop (Basics) (**photo j**), then hang the pendant on a cord.

[3] For a partially pierced pendant bead, cut the 19-gauge wire to 4 in. (10cm). Glue the wire into the partially pierced pendant, then string a spacer, an oval bead, and a 4mm bead. Make a wrapped loop, then hang the pendant on a cord.

[4] For earrings, cut two 4-in. strips of 20-gauge wire. Make a flattened spiral with the wire as in step 1, then string a 3mm bead, the polymer-clay earring bead, a spacer, and an oval bead. Finish by shaping the wire into an ear hook (**photo k**) and file the ends.

EDITOR'S NOTE: If you don't want to make your own wire findings, substitute 4-in. (10cm) head pins and purchased ear wires.

MATERIALS

- 4 2-oz. (56g) pkgs. Sculpey SuperFlex Bake & Bend modeling compound, any color
- sprigs of fresh foliage or individual leaves
- 2 2-oz. pkgs. (56g) Premo Sculpey, black
- Translucent Liquid Sculpey (TLS)
- Pearl Ex Pigment Powders, assorted colors
- 3 5 x 7mm beads
- 3 3 x 8mm metallic spacers
- 4mm metallic bead
- 2 3mm metallic beads
- 6 in. (15cm) 19-gauge gold wire
- 8 in. (20cm) 20-gauge wire
- Buna cord or other black rubber cord

TOOLS & SUPPLIES

- pasta machine*
- toaster or convection oven*
- cornstarch
- craft knife
- sanding sponge, coarse grit
- needle file
- paintbrush
- roundnose pliers
- wire cutters
- ballpeen hammer and anvil
- cyanoacrylate glue (optional)

*Dedicated to nonfood use

PENDANTS

Mystic collage

Combine rubber stamps, colored pencils, and polymer clay to unleash the artist within

by **Mari O'Dell**

By manipulating rubber-stamped images with a photocopy machine, it is possible to create a nearly endless supply of design elements. A group of insect wings might combine to construct a wonderful column; an open window might reveal a world filled with floating flowers. Ordinary images can take on a mysterious, almost mystic, quality when formed into a collage, bringing questions to mind: What do the symbols mean? What story is the artist telling? What is she trying to *say*?

After creating a collage and photocopying it at the desired size for your pin, you then add another layer of imagery by coloring it with easy-to-use colored pencils. The image is transferred to unbaked polymer clay, and then baked, which fixes the image. Finish the pin with black clay, beads, and gold leaf, and you've got a miniature mystery to wear or give.

Create your image

[1] Gather your rubber stamps, clip art, and drawings. Stamp images and manipulate them by enlarging and reducing on a copy machine. You'll use these pieces to create a collage. Remember, you don't have to use an entire image. Cut things away, white them out, or add lines with black marker. After you've manipulated images to a design you like, cut them out and glue or tape them in place on a blank sheet of paper. Make a photocopy of your collage. Reduce or enlarge as desired; the size you use will be the size your pin will be.

[2] Once you have a good plain-paper photocopy, color it with good-quality colored pencils (**photo a**). Blends and shaded colors look good on the finished work. Set the colored collage aside.

Make the pin

[1] Run ½ oz. (14g) of well-conditioned translucent Sculpey III on a medium setting of your pasta machine. Place the slab on a clean piece of flat mat board or other sturdy, movable surface.

[2] Trim the colored copy to the desired pin shape. Add a ¼-in. (6mm) border around the image to accommodate the trim edge that you'll add later.

[3] Turn the copy face down onto the translucent polymer clay and burnish in place. Trim the excess clay around the paper (**photo b**). Set the piece aside for at least 15 minutes to give the plasticizer time to leach the image from the paper. Leave the clay on the board so you can carry it around without disturbing the clay. Meanwhile, preheat the oven to the manufacturer's suggested temperature.

[4] Bake the paper, clay, and mat board in the oven for 15–20 minutes. After you take them out of the oven, carefully remove the paper from the clay (**photo c**). Let the piece cool.

[5] Using well-conditioned black Premo Sculpey, run ½ oz. (14g) through the pasta machine on the medium setting to make a backing sheet. Set it aside on tracing paper.

[6] Create another sheet of black Premo and attach a sheet of composition gold leaf to it by slowly peeling away the backing paper as you roll the leaf onto the clay. Burnish the leaf to the surface. Then run the leafed clay through the pasta machine once more

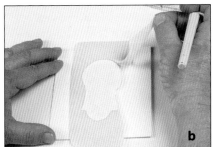

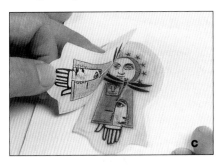

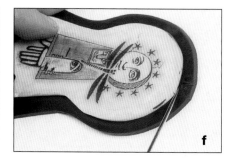

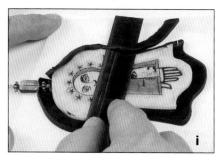

MATERIALS

- 2-oz. pkg. (56g) Premo Sculpey III, translucent
- 2-oz. pkg. (56g) Premo Sculpey, black
- plain-paper black-and-white photocopy of collage
- rubber stamps, clip art, drawings
- sheet composition gold leaf
- goldtone head pin and a few beads (optional)
- pinback

TOOLS & SUPPLIES

- pasta machine*
- toaster or convection oven*
- quality colored pencils (such as Prismacolor)
- craft knife
- tissue blade
- smooth-surface mat board
- wooden burnishing tool
- transparent tape or white glue
- tracing paper
- Zap-A-Gap cyanoacrylate glue

*Dedicated to nonfood use

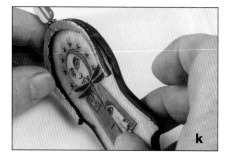

on the medium setting. Cut into ¼-in. (6mm) strips and set them aside on tracing paper (**photo d**).

[**7**] Place the sheet of plain black clay on a piece of mat board and put the translucent transfer piece on top. Trim, leaving about a ¾-in. (1.9cm) border of clay around the entire shape (**photo e**).

[**8**] Mark the placement for a beaded embellishment, if desired, as well as the top of the translucent piece (**photo f**). Remove the translucent piece.

[**9**] Thread a few beads on the head pin, lay it in position on the backing, and press it in place. Cover the bare metal with a piece of black clay run through the pasta machine on a thin-

ner setting and press it down (**photo g**).

[**10**] Replace the translucent piece. Slice the backing clay on each side of the bead embellishment down to the baked collage piece. Then fold up the edge of the backing clay, pressing it against the side of the baked piece (**photo h**).

[**11**] With a tissue blade, trim the backing clay so it is level with the baked piece (**photo i**). Trim off the clay behind the beaded embellishment.

[**12**] Roll the sides of the piece against tissue-covered mat board until they adhere well (**photo j**). Re-trim as needed.

[**13**] Place the piece face up on the mat board and lay a strip of leafed clay

along the top edge. It must also touch the unbaked clay edge (**photo k**). Press it in place.

[**14**] As you continue framing the piece with strips of leafed clay, you can miter joins or cover them with strapping pieces (**photo l**). Lift the unleafed cut edges and make sure they adhere to each other. If you wish, add small cane slices.

[**15**] Place the piece face down on the mat board and bake it in a preheated oven at the manufacturer's recommended temperature for 25 minutes. After it is cool, attach a pinback to the top third or higher, using Zap-A-Gap glue.

Uncommon combination

Pair polymer clay with dichroic glass

by **Janis Holler**

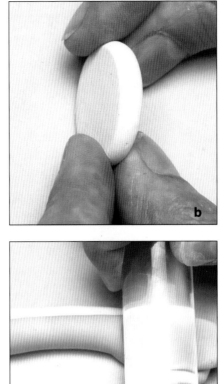

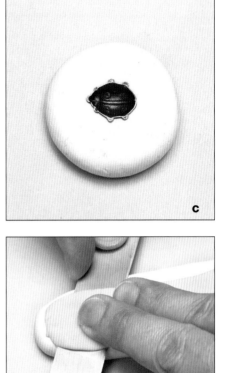

Embellishing dichroic glass with polymer clay isn't difficult, but to get long-lasting, wearable results, you must pay attention to the placement and anchoring of the polymer-clay elements. To create your own embellishments, begin by making a polymer-clay mold from one or two textured objects. For this project, a brass ladybug and a twig formed a nature-themed duo for embellishments (**photo a**). If you use a similar scheme, plan for one small and one large element to keep the scale of the design proportional.

Make the molds
[1] Condition a small lump of scrap clay (see Basics, p. 5). Roll it into a ball that is approximately ½ in. (1.3cm) in diameter.
[2] Flatten the ball into a ⅛-in.-thick (3mm) disk that is about 1 in. (2.5cm) in diameter (**photo b**). Lightly dust the top of the ladybug (or your small object) with baby powder or cornstarch, which acts as a release. Press the object top side down into the clay disk (**photo c**). Gently remove it.

[3] Repeat steps 1–2 with an oblong piece of scrap clay to create a mold for the twig (or your large object) (**photo d**).
[4] Bake the molds flat side down, following the manufacturer's directions for the type of clay used. To make the mold durable, don't skimp on the length of time you bake it.

Make the polymer-clay components
[1] Condition a small amount of bone polymer clay to make the twig (or use an appropriate color for your large object). Use your hands to roll it into a log that is long enough to cover the mold. Dust the mold with baby powder. Place the log on the mold and use a brayer or an acrylic rod to flatten it into the mold (**photo e**).
[2] Use a tissue blade to slice the excess clay from the mold (**photo f**). If needed, make a second pass with the blade to trim the remaining excess clay (**photo g**).
[3] To remove the raw-clay twig from the mold, lightly press some excess clay

on the twig in the mold. As long as the clay is not powdered, the two pieces should adhere to each other so the clay twig can be removed without damage.
[4] Use a craft knife to trim the excess clay from the twig edges (**photo h**).
[5] Repeat steps 1–4 to make a ladybug from red polymer clay (or an appropriate color for your small object).

Apply the components to the glass
Adhering the clay to the glass is not difficult as long as there is good contact between the two. While it is possible to adhere the clay without a "glue" such as Translucent Liquid Sculpey (TLS), it's recommended for added durability. Handle the polymer-clay elements as little as possible so they do not become too warm and soft.
[1] Determine where to put the twig (or your large object). Move it around on the dichroic glass until you find a pleasing arrangement, which will vary from pendant to pendant. Cut off the

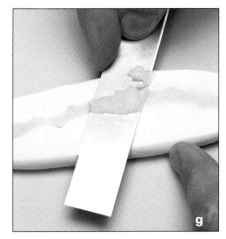

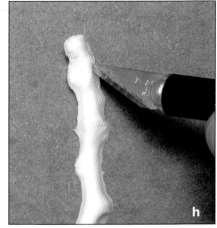

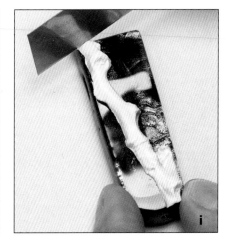

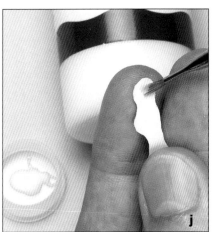

excess twig with a tissue blade or a craft knife (**photo i**) and use it on the back of the pendant as shown on the top right, p. 63. Then decide where to put the ladybug (or your small object). Remove the polymer-clay components from the glass.

[2] Squeeze a little TLS into a container. Use a small brush to lightly paint it onto the back of the twig. Cover the twig completely, but not excessively (**photo j**).

[3] Reposition the twig (or large object) as determined in step 1. Gently but firmly press it onto the surface of the glass. Don't press so hard that you either smash the twig or leave fingerprints in the clay. Use the brush to wipe up any excess TLS along the edge of the twig (**photo k**).

[4] Repeat steps 2–3 for the ladybug (or small object) and the leftover piece on the back of the pendant, or attach the back piece after baking the front attachments.

[5] Place the pendant on its side or prop it in the oven so that the clay will not be smudged during baking. Bake according to the manufacturer's directions.

Apply finishing touches

Use a dark color acrylic paint and a small paintbrush to antique the textured areas of the clay to bring out detail. Apply the paint. When it is partially dry, rub the excess off the surface of the clay with a soft cloth.

MATERIALS
- Premo Sculpey, 1 oz. (28g) each of the following colors: bone and red
- scrap polymer clay
- twig or other large object
- ladybug pin or button or other small object
- dichroic glass pendant
- Translucent Liquid Sculpey (TLS)
- acrylic paint, dark color

TOOLS & SUPPLIES
- pasta machine*
- toaster or convection oven*
- tissue blade
- baby powder or cornstarch
- brayer or acrylic roller
- craft knife
- paintbrushes for TLS and acrylic paint

*Dedicated to nonfood use

Imagine the possibilities

Anything goes when you transfer images onto polymer-clay pendants

by **Nancy Pollack**

Doodle a design. Snap a shot. Or pick a posy. Gather just about any object that fits on a photocopy machine and transform it into one-of-a-kind jewelry. The key to this project is Lazertran Silk transfer paper, which allows you to place your favorite image on polymer clay. Lazertran Silk offers two advantages over other transfer methods: The image is flexible, since you apply it to unbaked clay, and the clay thickness is variable. By incorporating your personal preferences, you create a polymer pendant that reflects your individual style.

Prepare the image

The geometric pattern shown on the pendant on p. 66 was created using Adobe *Photoshop Elements*. This software allows you to create images and manipulate drawings. After completing a design, print it or save the work on a disk. If you don't want to use a computer, select sketches, photos, or flat objects for your pendant image.

[1] Take the design items and Lazertran Silk sheets (**photo a**) to your local photocopy store. Request a reproduction to be made onto the shiny side of the Lazertran Silk. If your image has text, or if the orientation is otherwise important, have the technician copy it as a mirror image.

[2] Cut the images out of the Lazertran Silk sheet with a craft knife (**photo b**). If you need to crop an image, try doing this by eye or using a template such as a Zoomfinder or Shapelets. If using a template, place it on the image and move it around until you are satisfied with the design, then cut it out. Set the cut-out images aside.

Transfer the image to clay

[1] Condition ½ oz. (14g) of the white polymer clay (see Basics, p. 5).

[2] Run the conditioned clay through a pasta machine set on a medium-thin setting. The slab of clay should be 1 in. (2.5cm) larger than your image. If the slab is too small, condition a larger portion of clay and run it through the pasta machine. For a thicker, heavier pendant, set the machine to a slightly wider setting.

[3] Place the image face down on the middle of the clay sheet. Use a bone folder to burnish the image onto the clay (**photo c**). Make sure the entire image is in contact with the clay. Inadequate rubbing will cause white spots on your transfer.

[4] Leave the image on the clay for at least 30 minutes. (The more time the better.)

[5] Fill a pan with enough water to immerse the piece. Place the clay, image up, in the water. Allow it to soak for two minutes. Swish the water until the paper backing floats off the clay. If parts of the backing remain

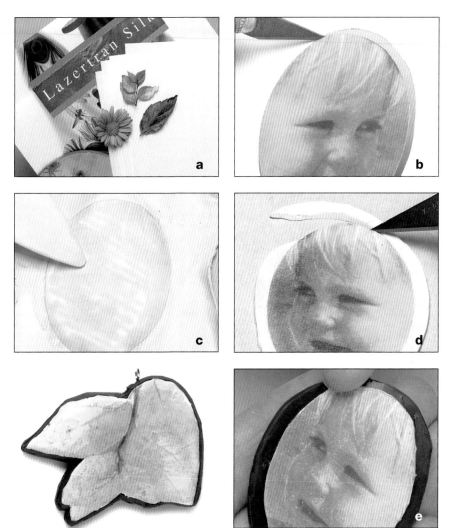

attached, do not peel off the paper; let the piece soak longer before swirling the water again.

[6] Remove the clay from the water; hold the piece over the pan and carefully tilt it to drip water off the clay.

[7] Set the piece on smooth coated paper such as deli, parchment, or waxed. Allow the image to air-dry as long as possible, at least one hour. A long drying period will make the piece more durable and resistant to damage from accidental contact. The image should not have any water droplets on it nor should it feel sticky when thoroughly dry.

Build the clay body

[1] Cover your work surface with clean paper. Place the clay, image up, on the paper.

[2] Using a craft knife, trim the dry clay piece to within ⅛ in. (3mm) of the image.

[3] Make a bevel cut around the edge of

the image (**photo d**), undercutting the edge so that the surface is larger than the bottom. This undercutting will help the image settle into the next layer.

[4] Condition approximately ½ oz. (14g) of black clay (or other complementary color) for the second layer. There will be a total of three or more layers.

[5] Run the conditioned clay through a pasta machine on a medium setting or your preferred thickness. The sheet of clay should be 1 in. larger than your image.

[6] Place the image on the second sheet. Trim the second layer to within ⅛ in. (3mm) of the image. Carefully smooth down the image's beveled edges, pressing with your fingernail (**photo e**). Or place deli, parchment, or waxed paper over the image and smooth the beveled edges with your fingernail on top of the paper.

[7] Bevel the edge of the bottom layer (**photo f**). This time, however, angle

MATERIALS

- Premo Sculpey, 2-oz. (56g) pkg. each of the following colors: white and black or other complementary color (optional)
- Lazertran Silk transfer sheets (lazertran.com)
- image or objects to be photo-copied
- Translucent Liquid Sculpey (TLS)
- eye pin
- bail
- chain

TOOLS & SUPPLIES

- color photocopier or toner-based laser printer
- pasta machine*
- toaster or convection oven*
- computer with Adobe *Photoshop Elements* (Adobe.com) (optional)
- craft knife or tissue blade
- Zoomfinder or Shapelets (polymerclayexpress.com) (optional)
- bone folder
- paper: deli, parchment, or waxed
- baking pan*
- Zap-A-Gap cyanoacrylate glue

*Dedicated to nonfood use

your craft knife in the opposite direction from step 3; henceforward, each layer should be wider than the previous one.

[8] If you choose to have more than three layers of clay, repeat steps 4–7. The pendants above have three layers, but the pendant shown on p. 66 uses six layers – including a layer of scrap clay hidden under the first layer – which gives it more dimension.

Finish the pendant

[1] Turn the pendant over, image side down. Make a recess in the back of the pendant with an eye pin (**photo g**). Make sure that the "eye" will come up high enough above the top of the pendant to attach the bail. Remove the eye pin.

[2] Bake the clay in an oven or toaster oven at 275°F (130°C) for 30 minutes, image side up. Baking may vary if you use a polymer clay other than Premo, so follow the manufacturer's directions.

[3] While the clay is baking, attach the bail to the eye pin.

[4] After the piece has finished baking and is cool, apply a small amount of Zap-A-Gap glue to the eye pin. Position the finding in the recess, making sure the eye pin and the bail are in the proper position.

[5] Condition more clay for the final layer. Roll a sheet at the medium setting or the preferred thickness. The sheet must be thick enough to hide the outline of the eye pin. To help the unbaked clay stick to the baked clay, put a little Translucent Liquid Sculpey (TLS) between the layers. Gluing is optional.

[6] Place the unbaked sheet onto the back of the pendant. Smooth it to eliminate any air bubbles. Turn the clay layers image side up. Trim and bevel the edges of the unbaked clay. Blend the edge into the baked clay.

[7] If you choose to add a border to the pendant, condition the clay and roll a sheet slightly thinner than your pendant. Cut the clay to the height and length of your pendant's edge, leaving extra length to ensure a proper fit. Wrap border clay around the edge of the pendant (**photo h**). Cut to the correct length. Press the border onto the pendant and smooth it onto the bottom clay layer, pressing with your fingernail (**photo i**) or a bone folder.

[8] Bake at 275°F (130°C) for 30 minutes or according to the manufacturer's directions.

[9] Remove the pendant from the oven. Thread the chain through the bail.

Polymer-clay lockets

Use polymer clay and an ordinary pinback to create these hinged treasures

by **Mike Buesseler**

Sophisticated and stylish, these lockets are a step beyond the traditional heart-shaped version that holds a tiny photo of one's sweetheart. Crisp, clean design lines demand a high level of finish to each variation, but the crowning touch is the top-hinged element, which lifts up to reveal the magnificent surprise inside.

The lockets can be made of any brand or type of polymer clay, but the examples shown here were all made with metallic or pearlescent Premo Sculpey, which produces the special shimmering effects. The general construction of the locket isn't particularly difficult or unique, except for the hinge, which is adapted from a high-quality pinback. Neatness counts with this project, so take your time on the finishing details.

Prepare the clay

[1] Choose two complementary colors of metallic clay. Condition the clay (see Basics, p. 5). Using a pasta machine, make a Skinner blend (Basics). Cut and construct the triangular pieces for a Skinner blend, but make them

MATERIALS

- approximately 2 oz. (56g) Premo Sculpey, two or more metallic colors for blending
- 2-oz. (56g) pkg. Premo Sculpey, black or other dark color
- good-quality pinback, 1 in. (2.5cm) or shorter
- head pin
- 4–5mm glass bead
- interesting cane slice

TOOLS & SUPPLIES

- pasta machine*
- toaster or convection oven*
- tissue blade
- needle tool
- Kemper or other clay cutters, ¾-in. (2cm) circle and one slightly smaller
- metal cutting pliers
- small drill and bit, 1/16-in. (1.6mm) diameter
- Zap-A-Gap cyanoacrylate glue

*Dedicated to nonfood use

narrow to keep the total width around 2 in. (5cm). As you make the blend, place one edge of the sheet you are blending against the edge of the pasta machine between the rollers. Use a tool or your thumbnail against the other edge to keep the width around 2 in.
[2] Once you have the sheet well blended, thin it with the pasta machine.

Construct the locket body

[1] Run a sheet of conditioned black or other dark-color clay on the thickest setting of the pasta machine. (Black and dark colors set off metallic colors nicely, but use whatever color works best for the design scheme you have in mind.) Cut the sheet into two pieces and stack them. The stack should be a little less than ¼ in. (6mm) thick. If desired, texture or embellish the stack's surfaces. Cut the stack into a rectangle about 1 x 2 in. (2.5 x 5cm) (**figure 1**).
[2] From this rectangle, cut out a locket shape. Design your own, or use one of the three shapes shown here (**figure 2**).
[3] Take the thin blended sheet from step 2 of the previous section and cut it to fit the size and shape of your locket design. Press or roll the sheet onto the face of the locket, making sure the sheet adheres tightly and removing any air bubbles trapped under it. Texture the surface of this blended sheet before baking. (Sheets of clay produced this way almost always bubble during baking. Texturing the sheet hides any bubbles and adds a nice effect to the finished piece. A Scotch Brite scouring pad was used on several of the lockets shown. Coarse sandpaper, window screen, or fabrics are a few other possibilities.)
[4] Use a ¾-in. (1.9cm) circle Kemper or other clay cutter to make a hole in the lower half of the locket body. Remove the clay (**figure 3**).

Make and add a pinback hinge

[1] Snip off about a third of the pin portion of the pinback (**figure 4**). Then cut off the clasp end of the pinback, leaving the tang less than ¾ in. (1.9cm)

long. The tang must be shorter than the diameter of the locket hole, so adjust accordingly if you are modifying these instructions.
[2] With a needle tool, make a small, shallow hole in the locket body, just below the top edge of the inside of the hole, to mark where the hinge will attach to the locket. Then push the remaining pin portion of the pinback into this hole (it will slide into the clay, even without the point). Push it in until the hinge is flush with the locket body (**figure 5**). Then remove the pinback from the locket body.
[3] Mark and remove a small amount of clay with a craft knife equal to the dimensions of the hinge itself. When you push the pinback back into the locket, the hinge will be flush with the inside of the hole in the body, and the tang will rotate up. Cut the hinge space out and reinsert the pinback to check the fit (**figures 6a and 6b**).
[4] With a ¾-in. (1.9cm) circle Kemper or other clay cutter, make a lid about ⅛ in. (3mm) thick from any color or blended color clay you like. The lids shown in this project are spirals, but many other designs are possible. You can embellish the lid however you want; just make sure it fits inside the locket hole (**figure 7**). Bake the lid and the locket pieces (with the pinback in place in the locket) according to the manufacturer's directions.
[5] After baking, check that the lid fits into the hole on top of the tang part of the pinback. Bend the tang and sand the lid if necessary to ensure a good fit (**figure 7**). (Wear a dust mask or work in a well-ventilated area to avoid inhaling polymer-clay dust.) Place some Zap-A-Gap or similar glue on the tang and press the lid into the hole on top of the tang until the glue sets. Then remove the lid and the attached pinback-hinge from the locket body.
[6] Cut out a thin piece of clay with a circle Kemper or other clay cutter that is the next size smaller. Press the circle of clay over the tang of the pinback where it is glued to the lid and rebake (**figure 8**). This finishing touch conceals the pinback when the lid is open.

Finish the locket

[1] To attach a bead as a handle to the lid, drill a small hole through the lid near its edge. Then insert a head pin through this hole from the underside (the side that will be inside the locket) and glue it in place. When the glue is dry, snip off most of the protruding end of the head pin, dab some glue on it, and slide a bead over the end (**figure 9**).

[2] Add finishing trim and findings to the locket. Since this may require additional bakings, do not glue the lid and hinge into the locket body until all other steps are complete. For the back of the locket, simply add a thin sheet (⅛ in./3mm or thinner) of black or other dark, complementary color over the back. This sheet will become the inside of the locket hole, so position an interesting cane slice or other embellishment to appear in the hole when the locket is open. Add thin slices of trim around the edges of the locket and rebake. Sand the finished locket with progressively finer grits of sandpaper for a smooth, professional presentation.

[3] When gluing the lid with its attached hinge to the locket body, take care not to use too much glue, or your hinge will freeze. Let just a little Zap-A-Gap glue get into the hinge, enough to make the lid open smoothly, but not so much that it tightens. This trick takes practice. If you get too much glue in the hinge, you can pull it out and reglue it, but it won't be easy.

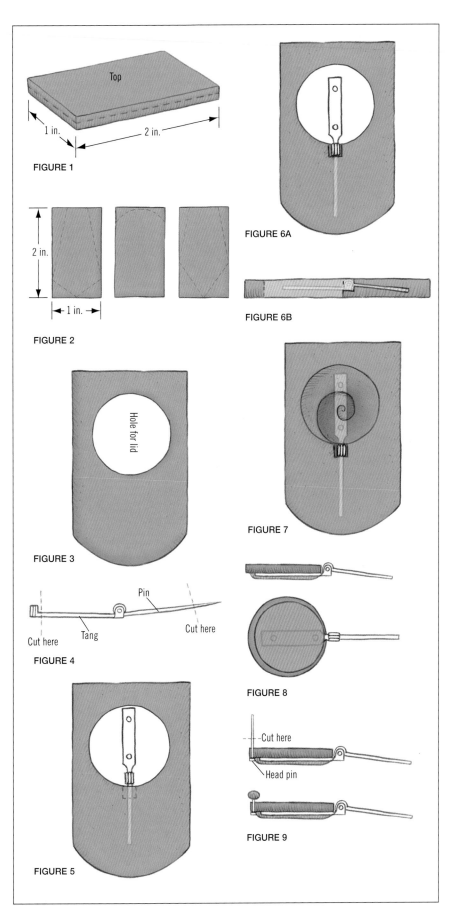

FIGURE 1

FIGURE 2

FIGURE 3

FIGURE 4

FIGURE 5

FIGURE 6A

FIGURE 6B

FIGURE 7

FIGURE 8

FIGURE 9

Elegant *inro* pendants

Form a Japanese pendant box with polymer clay

by **Carol Zilliacus**

Traditional Japanese *inro* boxes date back to the early 18th century. Because the Japanese kimono doesn't have pockets, belongings were often housed in containers and suspended from the *obi*, or sash. These *sagemono* varied in size and purpose; *inro*, for example, were very small nested boxes used to hold medicine or tobacco. Made of wood, bone, ceramic, or other materials, the wooden versions were often lacquered to a burnished gold.

The designs on the *inro* pendants here are made by layering sheets of two contrasting colors of polymer clay, then either slicing or carving a design in the top sheet to create a lacquered appearance. Use whichever method you prefer.

Prepare the clay
[1] Condition both colors of clay (see Basics, page 5). Run a 6 x 7-in. (15 x 18cm) sheet for the bottom layer through the pasta machine on the thickest setting. Roll the same size sheet for the top layer on a thinner setting.
[2] Stack the sheets together and roll lightly with a brayer or an acrylic rod to remove any air pockets.

Slice a design
The first option for creating a lacquered look is to cut the design with a craft knife. Use a new blade and tighten it firmly so it does not loosen when cutting curves. Before you begin slicing the prepared sheets, practice with two layers of scrap clay

to get a feel for how deeply you need to slice. Be sure both your hands and the clay are cold so you can make crisp cuts. If your workplace is warm, dunk your clay and tools in cold water.
[1] Plan a design for your clay. Make a drawing or look at a piece of artwork. Chinese and Japanese calligraphy provided the inspiration for many of the designs shown here.
[2] Lightly slice into the upper layer of clay with a craft knife to sketch out the design (**photo a**). Don't slice all the way through the first layer yet.
[3] After you have completed the design, begin slicing deeper to remove sections of the top layer (**photo b**). Cut across the beginning and end of curved

lines. Use a light touch at first. It's easy to slice deeper if your cut isn't complete.

[4] When you have completed your design, run the clay through the pasta machine on the thickest setting. The design will flatten and enlarge (**photo c**).

Carve a design

The second option for creating a lacquered look is to carve a design into the top layer. Dockyard's micro carving tools work great for delicate polymer-clay work, but you can use the instruments you prefer. Practice first on scrap clay.

[1] Repeat steps 1–2 of "Prepare the clay."

[2] Begin to carve out sections of clay according to your design (**photo d**). Be careful not to carve too deeply.

[3] Because carving often produces weak points in the embellished sheet, run a sheet the same color as the bottom layer through the pasta machine on a medium setting and line the back of the carved sheet to stabilize it.

[4] Repeat step 4 of "Slice a design."

Make the pendant body

[1] From cardstock, cut a 2¼ x 4-in. (5.7 x 10cm) rectangle to use as a template for the pendant body.

[2] Look at your embellished sheet and choose the most interesting section. Lay the template over this area and cut out the body section.

[3] Run a small sheet of clay through the pasta machine on a medium-thin setting. Cut a ¾ x 3-in. (1.9 x 7.6cm) strip. Place the strip so half of it is under one edge of the body section. Secure the bond with a few drops of Translucent Liquid Sculpey (TLS) and trim the strip so it is the same height as the body section (**photo e**). Curve the body section into an oval cylinder, abutting the edges over the clay strip. Roll a knitting needle against the outside and inside to ensure the layers adhere and to blend the seam.

[4] At this point, you can bake the cylinder according to the manufacturer's directions, placing it upright in the oven. You could work with raw clay through the whole construction process, but you might mar the embellished clay.

[5] Test the pendant body against the oval templates on page 74 to find the best size for the bottom. It should be slightly larger than the pendant's body. Trace the template on cardstock and cut it out. Fold it in quarters to find the center. Poke a hole in the center (**photo f**).

[6] Center the cylinder on the template and pierce holes to show where the sides should line up. Alternatively, you can jump to step 7 and cut out the clay oval, then center the cylinder directly on the oval by brushing a small amount of mica powder or cornstarch on the cylinder's bottom edge and placing the cylinder on the clay oval (**photo g**). The marks left behind will guide final placement.

[7] Use a blunt-end lace tool to cut out the bottom shape from the embellished clay sheet. Place the clay sheet on some smooth coated paper such as deli, parchment, or waxed. Rotate the template and clay sheet together on the paper, applying firm pressure with the lace tool to cut a perfect oval.

[8] Transfer the marks made on the template to the wrong side of the clay oval and pierce a hole in its center (**photo h**). Put a little TLS on the bottom of the cylinder and press it lightly in place on the oval, lining it up with the marks made on the clay. Gently tap the top of the cylinder to adhere it to the oval.

[9] Roll a thin snake of clay and place it around the bottom of the cylinder. Cut off any extra so the ends abut. Use the blunt end of the lace tool to press a pattern into the snake, which will also secure it to the join (**photo i**).

Make the lid

Unless you want a perfectly symmetrical design, choose a slightly larger oval template for the top.

[1] Repeat steps 6–7 of "Make the pendant body" for the pendant's lid.

[2] To make the interior or stopper portion of the lid, cut a 3 x ½-in. (7.6 x 1.3cm) strip of clay. Form the clay into an oval cylinder. Brush a thin coat of mica powder or cornstarch on the top inside of the pendant cylinder and test the fit of the stopper. The powder will prevent sticking. You may have to adjust the stopper size several times before it fits.

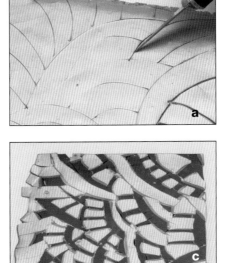
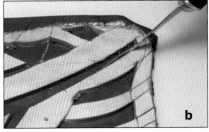

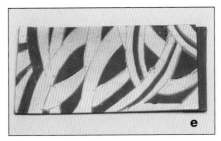

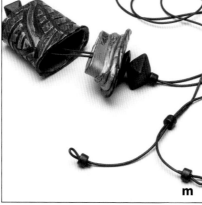

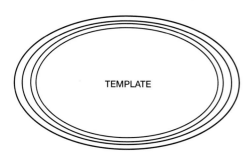

TEMPLATE

Cut off any extra clay so the ends abut smoothly.

[3] Center the stopper on the wrong side of the lid (**photo j**). Gently push down on the stopper so it binds to the top. Test the join by turning the lid over. If the stopper falls off, use a little TLS on the stopper to secure the join.

[4] Repeat step 9 of "Make the pendant body" to secure the join (**photo j**).

[5] Dust powder inside the top of the pendant body again. Fit the lid onto the pendant and place it on a baking sheet.

[6] Bake the clay pieces according to the manufacturer's directions for 30 minutes. After baking, submerge the pendant in cold water and gently press the pendant and top together to ensure a perfect fit.

Finish the pendant

[1] To create an antique, carved-wood look on the cutwork, rub a layer of burnt umber acrylic paint on the pendant (**photo k**). When the paint is dry, buff the pendant and lid separately with an electric buffer or by hand to give the pieces a satin glow. If you have a Dremel or Foredom flex-shaft, use that with a buffing attachment.

[2] Enlarge the holes on the bottom and the lid with a ⅛-in. (3mm) drill bit using a flex-shaft or power drill.

[3] Cut a 1½-yd. (1.4m) length of Buna cord. Trim the ends at an angle so they will be easy to thread through the beads.

[4] Center a mini-tube on the cord. String an oxyhedron and a round washer over both cord ends and up to the mini-tube. Pass both ends through the hole in the bottom of the pendant (**photo l**).

[5] Pass both ends through the hole in the lid from inside to outside. String a washer, an oxyhedron, and a mini-tube over both ends. String another mini-tube or an oxyhedron over both cords to serve as the clasp. Check the length of the necklace. Leave 4- to 8-in. (10–20cm) tails and trim excess cord if necessary. String a mini-tube on each cord 1 in. (2.5cm) from the end. Put a drop of Zap-A-Gap glue inside the tube bead and slip the end back into the bead, creating a ½-in. (1.3cm) loop (**photo m**).

MATERIALS

- Premo Sculpey, one 2-oz. (56g) pkg. each of the following colors: black and metallic gold
- Translucent Liquid Sculpey (TLS)
- acrylic paint, burnt umber (optional)
- ¹⁄₁₆-in. (1.2mm) Buna cord (polymerclayexpress.com)
- large-hole ceramic beads (mykonosbeads.com):
    5–6 6 x 4mm mini-tubes (RM)
    2–3 12 or 15mm oxyhedrons (K5 or K6)
    2 6 x 24mm round washers (R3 or R4)

TOOLS & SUPPLIES

- pasta machine*
- toaster or convection oven*
- brayer or acrylic rod
- craft knife
- index cards or cardstock
- mica powder or cornstarch
- paper: deli, parchment, or waxed
- blunt-end Kemper lace tool
- double-pointed knitting needle
- stiff NuBlade
- Dockyard micro carving tools, 3 or 4mm gauge
- flex shaft (Dremel or Foredom), ⅛ in. (3mm) drill bit, buffing attachment (optional)
- electric buffer (optional)
- Zap-A-Gap cyanoacrylate glue

*Dedicated to nonfood use

Stylish polymer-clay tassels

Embellish your jewelry or your home with these decorative tassels

by **Terry Lee Czechowski**

Lazertran Silk transfer paper imbues vivid color images onto unbaked clay, opening a realm of exciting design opportunities. (See "Imagine the Possibilities," page 66, for another project using this product.) The patterned pieces can be used for almost any project – in this case, tassel pendants. For something beyond

jewelry, use these techniques to create key tassels, light or fan pulls, small tiebacks, or almost any other home-décor application where a decorative tassel can add a bit of personal pizzazz.

Transfer an image

[1] Copy your image on a Lazertran Silk sheet with a toner-based color copier, fol-

lowing the manufacturer's directions. If the design has words or you want it to transfer exactly as is, you must start with a mirror image of the design. Any copy shop should be able to help you flip the image, if you don't have the necessary equipment at home. The basic tassel requires only a 2 x 3-in. (5 x 7.6cm) image, so plan three or four images to

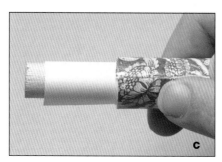

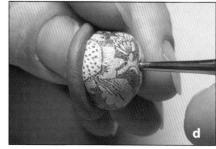

MATERIALS

- Fimo Soft, one 2-oz. (56g) pkg. each of the following colors: white or light color and black or accent color
- Transparent Liquid Sculpey (TLS)
- Sculpey Diluent
- Lazertran Silk (Lazertran.com)
- 2 x 3-in. (5 x 7.6cm) color image
- tassel or fibers for making a tassel
- 6 in. (15cm) 20-gauge craft wire
- 10–20 in. (25–50cm) cord for hanging tassel

TOOLS & SUPPLIES

- pasta machine*
- toaster or convection oven*
- craft knife
- wood burnishing tool
- sponge
- needle tool
- 4-in. (10cm) wood dowel, ½-in. (1.3cm) diameter
- chainnose and roundnose pliers
- waxed paper
- glue stick
- small circle cutter (optional)
- craft glue

*Dedicated to nonfood use

copy onto each LTS sheet so as not to waste the sheet. You may reduce your chosen image to an earring size and include two of those images on the sheet.

[2] Condition white or light-colored polymer clay (see Basics, p. 5) until it is soft and pliable.

[3] Run the clay through the pasta machine at a medium setting to make a sheet ⅛ in. (3mm) thick and larger than 2 x 3 in. (5 x 7.6cm).

[4] Place the sheet of clay on waxed paper. Rub a small amount of Sculpey Diluent on the clay until there is a bit of a drag on the clay's surface. The clay should not be slick or shiny. Blot up any excess.

[5] Cut the 2 x 3-in. image from the Lazertran Silk sheet and lay it face down on the clay. Burnish it thoroughly and gently to achieve complete contact between the image and the clay (photo a). Allow it to set for 15 minutes.

[6] With a damp sponge, blot the paper backing of the Lazertran Silk sheet image to release the adhesive (photo b). Wet the paper thoroughly. Blot up any excess water and gently lift the backing paper off the clay. (See "Transfer the image to clay," p. 67, for an alternate approach.)

Make a pendant

[1] Allow the transferred image to dry and cure for at least an hour or preferably overnight.

[2] Wrap a 3 x 4-in. (7.6 x 10cm) piece of paper around a wood dowel and use a glue stick to adhere the paper to itself, keeping glue off the exposed paper.

[3] Slice away excess clay from the transferred image. Carefully wrap the patterned clay around the paper on the dowel. Trim the clay so that the ends join neatly without an overlap (photo c). Blend the seam in gently.

[4] Bake the cylinder according to the manufacturer's directions. Allow it to cool.

[5] Roll two ½-in.-diameter (1.3cm) balls with black or accent clay. Flatten them into 1-in.-diameter (2.5cm) disks. Use a small circle cutter or craft knife to cut out the center of one disk to make a lip for the cylinder's bottom. (Alternatively, you can roll a thin snake of clay to apply as the cylinder's lip.)

[6] Roll another ½-in.-diameter (1.3cm) ball. Wrap the ball with a left-over scrap of the transfer-image clay or leave it plain. Cut the ball in half.

[7] Remove the baked cylinder from the dowel. Dab some Sculpey Diluent on both ends of the cylinder. If the clay becomes shiny, blot off the diluent.

[8] Attach the cut-out disk to the cylinder's bottom end. Center the half ball of clay onto the other disk and pierce a hole through the center of the ball and the disk (photo d). Press them securely onto the cylinder's other end.

[9] Bake the assembled pendant according to the manufacturer's directions.

Add a tassel

[1] Make a wrapped loop (Basics) at one end of the craft wire and tie the tassel to the wrapped loop. Dab some craft glue on the tassel top. Insert the wire into the cylinder and out the top hole. Pull the tassel snugly into the cylinder. Make another wrapped loop at the top. String the pendant on a cord. If you like, also make coordinating beads for the cord ends.

[2] For another option, eliminate the need for wire by piercing the top ball horizontally instead of vertically. Glue the tassel into the pendant and thread the cord through the hole in the ball (see the tassel, far left, page 75). Other options include embellishing the pendant with beads, metal foils, or extruded clay and adding beaded fringe or metallic fiber tassels.

Heart to heart

Your personal touch makes a heartfelt pendant percolating with personality

by **Christi Friesen**

Custom-colored polymer-clay pendants make engaging accessories and personalize any necklace. Make more than one, so you can give a heart away and hold on to another. The instructions here create one heart pendant, approximately 1½ in. (3.8cm) high. Adjust as necessary if you prefer a heart of a different size.

Winged heart (above left)
[1] Condition the clay (see Basics, p. 5).
[2] Mix the base color by combining ½ oz. (14g) of gold and ½ oz. (14g) of copper clay. Run the clay through your pasta machine until thoroughly blended.
[3] Cut a pea-size portion of the base clay, then mix it with the same amount of ecru clay and ½ oz. (14g) of gold clay. Set this accent color aside. Make a second accent color by blending ½ oz. (14g)

of gold clay with a pea-size portion of ecru; **photo a** shows the base color on bottom, accent colors on top.
[4] Mold the base clay into a teardrop (**photo b**), then cut a V at the wide end using a craft knife or tissue blade (**photo c**).
[5] Smooth the clay with your hands to form a heart shape and flatten slightly.
[6] Wrap a 3-in. (7.6cm) strip of 16- or 18-gauge wire around a pencil or needle tool. Pull the ends together using pliers (**photo d**).
[7] Wrap the wire loop with 22-gauge wire, starting at the loop's base and working down ¼ in. (6mm). Embed the ends of the wire into the V at the top of the heart (**photo e**).
[8] Make a dozen feather embellishments with each color of accent clay.

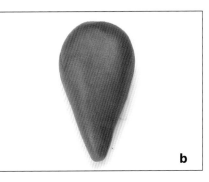

a

b

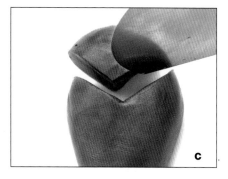

c

d

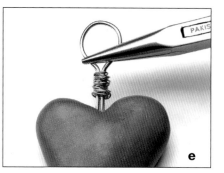

e

f

g

h

i

EDITOR'S NOTE: Craft stores sell Premo Sculpey in 2-oz. (56g) packages. The clay is segmented in four strips, like a scored candy bar – perfect for the ½-oz. (14g) needs of this project.

MATERIALS

- Premo Sculpey, 2-oz. (56g) pkg. each of the following colors: copper, gold, and ecru
- 3 3–5mm gemstones or pearls
- 10 in. (25cm) 22-gauge wire, dead soft
- 3–4 in. (7.6–10cm) 16- or 18-gauge wire, dead soft
- 6 in. (15cm) 28-gauge craft wire
- acrylic paint, burnt sienna and burnt umber (optional)
- Sculpey Glaze Satin or other clear varnish

TOOLS & SUPPLIES

- pasta machine*
- toaster or convection oven*
- craft knife or tissue blade
- needle tool
- flatnose or chainnose pliers
- wire cutters
- 2 index cards or cardstock
- paintbrush (optional)
- sponge (optional)
- baking sheet*

*Dedicated to nonfood use

Roll small balls of clay, then pinch them to resemble large grains of rice (**photo f**). [9] Press the rice-like embellishments on top of the heart, starting in the middle. Flatten the embellishments to resemble feathers (**photo g**). Overlap with alternating colors of clay and work your way to the top edge. [10] Drag a craft knife or needle tool over the center of the feathers to create shafts (**photo h**). [11] Center a pearl or gemstone on 2 in. (5cm) of 28-gauge wire. Twist the wire ends together using pliers. Continue until the wire twists firmly against the bead. Clip with wire cutters, leaving a ¼-in. (6mm) tail. Repeat with the remaining two beads. Press the wired beads into the heart (**photo i**). [12] Place the clay heart on cardstock and bake according to the manufacturer's directions. (These were baked at 275°F/135°C for 30 minutes.) Cool the clay. [13] Add an optional patina by painting the top of the heart with a mixture of burnt umber and burnt sienna acrylic paints. Apply paint to half of the top, then wipe with a damp sponge. Work quickly, so only the crevices retain the paint. [14] Whether you opted for the patina or not, coat the clay with a clear, protective glaze. Place the heart on clean cardstock and bake at 200°F (93°C) for 10 minutes to set the glaze.

Dotted heart (p. 77, right)

[1] Repeat steps 1–8 from "Winged heart," changing the clay color and twisting the wire loop as desired. [2] Embellish the heart with pearls, poke patterns with the needle tool, and add wire accents. [3] Repeat steps 11–14 from "Winged heart" to finish.

FAUX TECHNIQUES

By combining colors, adding texture, and sanding and polishing the end result, you can mimic many traditional art forms, such as *cloisonné* and porcelain, with polymer clay. Amazingly, you'll achieve remarkable results without special equipment or materials.

Faux cinnabar

Use molds to replicate classic Chinese pendants

by **Nan Roche**

Traditional cinnabar lacquerware is the term applied to reddish, highly carved, ornamental pieces, whether a small tray, vase, box, or some other *objet d'art*. A laborious process, some 200 to 500 coats of lacquer must be applied to an armature before the base is deep enough for carving. Lacquer does not dry like paint. Instead it hardens as it evaporates, and each layer must be applied and allowed to dry completely before the next coat can be added, a process that requires months or sometimes even years. Various shades of cinnabar are used to color each coat of lacquer, and the beauty of these gradations becomes apparent under the hands of a master carver when the piece is finally carved.

A similar effect is achieved with *mokume gane* (or "wood-grain metal"), a Japanese metalworking technique that has been adapted for use with polymer clay. By layering colors of clay and altering the surface's topography, different layers are revealed when the piece is carved or sanded. For this project, rather than carving the surface, the topography is created when the clay layers are pushed into a mold. The layers are then heavily sanded and polished. After the final polish, the object will look very much like old carved cinnabar lacquer.

To make this pendant, choose molds that are deeply cut and have fine detail. Soap-making molds work very well. Other good choices are wooden German cookie molds, antique butter molds, ceramic paper molds, and plastic and rubber molds created for use with polymer clay. You also can make your own molds from scrap clay by carving or taking an impression from found objects.

Make layered clay sheets

[1] Condition the black and red clays (see Basics, p. 5). Fold each clay sheet in half between each rolling and insert the clay fold first. The clay will spread to the width of the pasta machine, forming even rectangular sheets.
[2] Place the black and red sheets together and run them through the pasta machine on the widest setting.

[3] Cut this sheet in half and layer the halves so the colors alternate (**photo a**). Run this sheet through the pasta machine. Now the sheet has four layers. Repeat this step twice to create a 16-layer sheet.

Press the clay into a mold

[1] Before pressing the clay into a mold, decide which color, black or red, will dominate the finished piece. Each will produce a different result. For the samples shown here, the black surface faced the mold. Cut the layered clay sheet so it is a bit larger than the area of your mold.
[2] Prepare the clay surface by dusting a thin layer of cornstarch on the side that will be placed against the mold (**photo b**). Treating the clay instead of the mold prevents build-up of cornstarch in the mold and ensures that the clay is nonsticky everywhere. Apply cornstarch to the clay's opposite side and to your fingers to prevent sticking when you press the clay into the mold.
[3] Lay the clay in the mold with the preferred side down. First, press the clay into the mold's center and work out toward the edges. Press firmly with your thumbs to ensure the clay is forced into all the depressions. If needed, press small pieces of scrap clay into any deep depressions. Use scrap

clay to build a level surface on the piece's back before removing it from the mold (**photo c**).
[4] Remove the clay from the mold by gently pulling up the edges around the mold's perimeter. If you detect sticking, work gently on another area, coaxing the clay sheet from the mold.

Apply the backing

[1] Trim the excess clay from the molded clay's edges with a craft knife, beveling the edge toward the underside of the piece. Lay the piece face up on your work surface and slice around the perimeter, tipping the blade toward the inside of the piece (**photo d**).
[2] After the piece is trimmed, round the edges toward the back with your fingers. Because the sheet is layered, cutting it reveals stripes. Rounding the clay creates a nicely finished edge of one color.

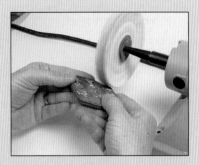

Buffing tips

Buffing machines can be dangerous. Always wear eye protection and keep long hair pinned up out of the way. Always hold your piece with both hands. Place the piece against the lower third of the wheel. Move it around continuously to avoid hot spots, which will partially re-melt polymer clay. Be sure to have a box or other barrier behind the wheel in case your piece flies out of your hands at high speed, something that is almost certain to happen from time to time.

The buffer shown here is a Foredom variable-speed buffing machine with a 4 x 30 sewn muslin buff and a 4 x 50 Star buff wheel. If you prefer not to invest in a stationary buffer, you can buy buff wheels for use in flex-shafts such as Dremel's or even your power drill.

For best success without a machine, sand your piece with progressively finer grits of wet/dry sandpaper – for instance, progressing from 320-, to 400-, to 600-, to 1000-, and finally to 1500-grit. This may seem tedious but it is the only way to achieve a mirror-smooth finish. Use a piece of old denim cloth to give a final hand polish to the piece.

[3] Run a sheet of well-conditioned black clay through the pasta machine on the middle setting. Use a piece of very coarse sandpaper (such as 36-grit) to texture the black sheet's surface (**photo e**). Be sure to use cornstarch as a release before burnishing the sandpaper into the clay.

[4] Lay the black sheet textured side down and place the molded piece on top of it. Secure the textured backing to the clay by pressing the two pieces together. Trim off the excess clay backing and smooth the edges between the front and back of the piece with your fingers (**photo f**). Use the sandpaper to re-texture the areas that you smoothed with your fingers, if necessary.

[5] Bake the piece according to the manufacturer's directions.

Sand and polish

After baking, finish the piece by sanding with wet/dry sandpaper starting with 220-grit, then 320-, 400-, and finally, 600-grit. Finish by buffing with a buffing machine (see "Buffing Tips," above). If you don't have a buffer, continue to sand your pieces with 1000- and 1500-grit wet/dry sandpaper and use a piece of old denim to hand polish.

String the necklace

Drill a hole in your work after

baking in order to create an even-sized hole that the rubber cording will fit into tightly. You can use anything from a power drill (a bit oversized for jewelry work, but usable) to flex-shafts to small cordless drills, to hand push drills. Simply pick a bit that matches the diameter of your cording. Rubber O-ring material is strong, soft to the touch, easy to cut and glue, and doesn't compete with the polymer-clay pieces like shiny metal findings would.

[1] Mark your piece where you want

each cord end to enter. Since you will glue the cord in place, you do not need to drill a hole that goes through the entire piece, but make sure the holes look symmetrical.

[2] Carefully drill a hole at each marking about ¼ in. (6mm) deep. Apply a drop of cyanoacrylate glue on a cord end and insert it in the hole. Repeat with the other cord end.

MATERIALS
- Premo Sculpey, one 2-oz. (56g) pkg. each of the following colors: black and cadmium red
- rubber cording, 0.103 diameter (available from I.B. Moore, 606-255-5501)

TOOLS & SUPPLIES
- pasta machine*
- toaster or convection oven*
- deeply cut soap or cookie molds of wood, ceramic, metal, or plastic*
- soft-bristled brush
- cornstarch

- craft knife
- coarse 36-grit sandpaper
- drill and #37 drill bit (to correspond to rubber cording)
- wet/dry sandpaper, in 220-, 320-, 400-, and 600-grit
- scrap of old denim
- cyanoacrylate glue, gel form (Loctite brand recommended)
- buffing machine (optional)
- wet/dry sandpaper, in 1000- and 1500-grit (optional)

*Dedicated to nonfood use

Faux lacquer brooches

Combine rubber-stamped images,
PolyShrinks, and polymer clay
for something spectacular

by **Mari O'Dell**

FAUX TECHNIQUES

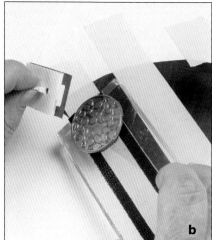

Risking rejection and going for something that you really want is often the only way wonderful things can happen for you. Similarly, experimenting with materials and combining things that aren't supposed to go together can produce fabulous messes – or exciting and remarkable results. That's how these faux lacquer pins came about.

This project combines several crafting disciplines into one piece of art. Pull out your favorite rubber stamps, a few PolyShrink plastic sheets, some colored and metallic inks, and – of course – polymer clay. Very soon, you'll have something special to wear or to give.

Create the PolyShrink base

[1] Sand a piece of black PolyShrink with 400-grit sandpaper horizontally and vertically on both sides. Remove dust with a paper towel.

[2] Make a shape or pattern that is 40–50 percent larger than what you want your finished size to be and trace it onto the PolyShrink (photo a). Cut it out with scissors or a craft knife.

[3] Use small pieces of masking tape to secure the pattern to a piece of blank paper. Then stamp images on the piece with colored and metallic inks. The brooches shown in this project were stamped lightly with an Encore Metallic Ink and then Colorbox Crafter's Colors were blended on top (photo b), but you can use the products you prefer. Work from the center out, masking areas and stamping or adding bands of color by stamping with a brush pad (photo c). Be careful not to smear the ink; it isn't permanent until sealed with clear embossing powder (step 5, below).

[4] Place the stamped PolyShrink shape on a piece of mat board and put it in a pre-heated 275°F (135°C) oven. Be patient. In 2–8 minutes, the plastic will shrink and curl; then it will thicken and lie flat. Remove from the oven and allow to cool. If the edges curl slightly, weight the plastic with a heavy book until it is cool.

[5] Now for the exciting part! Sprinkle the top of the shrink plastic with clear embossing powder (photo d). Smooth the edges and remove extra powder on the edges with your fingers. Carefully replace the piece on the mat board and put it back in the 275°F (135°C) oven. Watch the powder become clear and then liquid. Keep watching, and when the surface is smooth, remove it from the oven. Do not let the board tip or

d

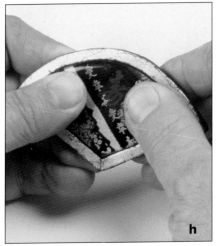

h

A shrink-plastic ruler

Different kinds and colors of PolyShrink shrink at different rates, so if you want to work with this medium, make a shrink-plastic ruler to gauge the size of your finished lacquer pieces.

Start by sanding a piece of black PolyShrink and then cutting a 2-in.-wide (5cm) strip off along the 10½-in. (26.7cm) edge. Use a ruler to mark fourth, half, and whole inches with a white or gold paint marker. Then shrink according to the manufacturer's directions, putting the PolyShrink on a piece of mat board to slow the shrinkage and prevent warping. After shrinking, the ruler will show the size of a measured piece of PolyShrink after heating.

MATERIALS

- sheet of black PolyShrink (luckysquirrel.com)
- assorted rubber stamps
- Encore Metallic Inks, Colorbox Crafter's Inks, or assorted inks of choice
- clear embossing powder
- 2 2-oz. (56g) pkgs. Sculpey III or Premo Sculpey, black
- composition gold leaf
- pinback

TOOLS & SUPPLIES

- pasta machine*
- toaster or convection oven*
- scissors or craft knife
- tissue blade
- masking tape
- 3–4 blank sheets of paper; tracing paper
- smooth-surfaced mat board
- spoon*
- 400-grit sandpaper
- Zap-A-Gap cyanoacrylate glue

*Dedicated to nonfood use

the molten embossing powder will run off the PolyShrink. Allow it to cool completely (**photo e**). The clear embossing powder on top of the colorized PolyShrink creates an effect similar to lacquer in appearance.

Make the pin
[1] Run two sheets of well-conditioned black polymer clay (see Basics, p. 5) through the pasta machine at a medium setting (¼ in./6mm thick).
[2] Take one sheet of the black clay and attach it to a piece of composition gold leaf as follows: Open the book of leaf, exposing a single sheet, and place the polymer-clay sheet carefully on top. Gently press down, then pick up the piece of clay with the leaf attached and place it on your work surface. Smooth the surface of the leaf,

burnishing it to the clay. Then run it through the pasta machine at the medium setting again. Place it on a sheet of tracing paper and set aside.
[3] Make a template of the desired finished size and shape of the pin. The template should allow for a gold-leafed polymer-clay border ¼–½ in. (6mm–1.3cm) all the way around the perimeter of the PolyShrink piece. Using the template, cut out a backing piece from the unleafed sheet of clay. Center the PolyShrink piece on top.
[4] Use a tissue blade to cut ¼- to ½-in.-wide strips of gold-leafed clay. Ease the leafed strips in place and abut the PolyShrink piece. Do not overlap (**photo f**). Miter the corners if desired and trim the edges. Press the strips into the clay base and smooth the edges.

[5] Pop the PolyShrink piece out of the clay frame without distorting the frame (**photo g**). Place the polymer-clay frame on mat board and bake it in a 265°F (130°C) oven for 25–30 minutes. Allow to cool.
[6] Dot the back of the PolyShrink piece with Zap-A-Gap glue and hold it in place in the base for 30 seconds (**photo h**). Sand the back of the pin finding and the back of the pin where it will go. Apply glue to the pinback and hold it in place 30–40 seconds. If the pinback is moved even a fraction, the glue will not bond. If this happens, sand both pieces and try again.

Faux enamel

Add dabs of gold leaf and intense color to enrich a textured polymer-clay pendant

by Patricia Kimle

Enameling has been a part of jewelry-making for centuries, though today the process is now more commonly used on everyday household products to make them more durable – just look at the surface of your appliances or the inside of your washing machine. In the jewelry world, enameling fuses layers of colored glass onto metal, and the piece must be fired each time a new color is applied, which takes a lot of heat.

Classic decorative enameling techniques include *cloisonné*, which outlines areas to be filled with enamel, and *impasto*, which builds up layers for relief designs. This project approximates the look of impasto enamel by texturing polymer clay, applying 23K gold leaf, saturating the surface with color, and finishing the piece with a coat of thick epoxy resin. One big benefit of taking this approach is that this faux enamelwork in polymer clay can be baked once at a mere 275°F (135°C), not fired multiple times at 1500°F (815°C), as required for true enamel.

Form the pendant

[1] Using scrap clay, form the pendant's core by making a rough shape approximately ¼ in. (6mm) thick in the desired diameter. One side should be flat and the other side should have a smooth beveled curve (**photo a**). A circle cutter may be helpful in shaping.

[2] Bake the pendant form, following the manufacturer's directions for the type of scrap clay you used.

Make the leaf impression mold

[1] Run the Sculpey SuperFlex Bake & Bend modeling compound through a pasta machine set to medium thickness. Aim for a setting slightly greater than your machine's center option.

[2] Cut a sheet of the rolled clay about 1 in. (2.5cm) larger on all sides than the leaf to be molded. Apply corn-starch liberally to the modeling compound's surface, removing all stickiness. Carefully place the leaf on the surface (**photo b**). Run the leaf and sheet together through the pasta machine on the medium setting. Carefully peel the leaf off the modeling compound and check the design (**photo c**). If the leaf shifted too much or if the impression is not what you want, knead the compound and try again. When you have the desired results, bake the leaf mold following the manufacturer's directions.

Add a stamped border

[1] Condition the gold polymer clay (see Basics, p. 5) and run it at the medium setting. Impress a strip of the clay with the rubber stamp border design.

[2] Trim one side close to the border. Position that edge over about one-third of the pendant form. Add a light coat of Translucent Liquid Sculpey (TLS) to the area you will cover on the form, then set the clay border layer in place on top. Trim the round outside edge (**photo d**).

Add the leaf

[1] Powder the remaining gold clay sheet with cornstarch. Lay the clay on your leaf mold (**photo e**). Run them together through the pasta machine's widest setting.

[2] Rotate the sheet of embossed gold clay until you find a pleasing orientation of the leaf impression. Trim a straight edge so you can place the piece next to the border design on the pendant form.

[3] Add a light coat of TLS to the area you will cover on the form, then set the leaf section in place on top (**photo f**). Trim the round outside edge.

Position and set the gold leaf

[1] From the gold leaf sheet, trim a piece large enough to cover the pendant form (**photo g**). Lay the sheet over the pendant with the tissue paper side up. Rub the tissue paper side gently until it separates from the gold.

[2] Using a soft bristled brush, gently tap and smooth the gold onto the surface of the clay (**photo h**). Tiny fractures will appear where the gold won't stretch into depressions in the clay. If any fractures appear too large, trim additional pieces of leaf from your original sheet and add them to the bare spots following the same method.

Finish the pendant

[1] Bake the pendant form for about 15 minutes or following the manufacturer's directions.

[2] On a palette, squeeze out several dime-size pools of TLS. Make a pool for each color of Piñata Ink you intend to use. Add and stir in a single drop of ink per pool (**photo i**). Keep colors separate. Let the palette rest for at least 30 minutes.

[3] Using the tip of the palette knife, carefully touch one color of the TLS/ink to the recesses of the border design (**photo j**). Take

Gauging thickness

It's not always easy to know the thicknesses of the various settings on your pasta machine. Usually a precise thickness isn't critical to a project, but sometimes it is – such as when you are trying to make a mold. In such instances, you need a width thick enough to allow for the molded item's depth. Here's a way to determine the settings on your pasta machine.

Condition some SuperFlex Bake & Bend modeling compound. Roll a sheet you estimate will be about half the thickness you want for your impression mold. Fold the compound in half. Run the compound through your pasta machine on its thickest setting. If your estimate is correct, the length should increase by about 10 percent. If your doubled length doesn't stretch at all, the compound will be too thin for you to get a good impression. If it stretches more than 10 percent, your setting will be too thick.

Once you have a sense of how thick the compound should be for the impression mold, reset the machine to the next step thicker than the middle setting. Do not fold the modeling compound when you run it through to make the impression. If your mold does not turn out deep and clear, rework the compound, adjust to a thinner setting, and run it through again.

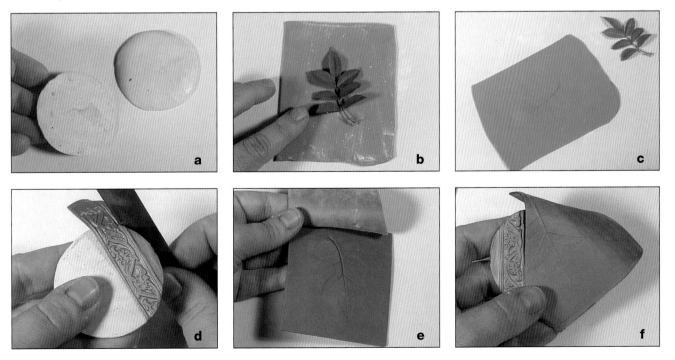

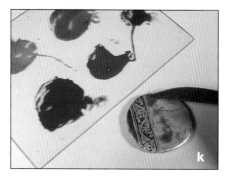

care to keep the raised surfaces clean. Use a shaping tool tipped with rubber or a cotton swab to wipe away smears.

[4] Set the color by holding a heat gun close to the piece for a few seconds until the shine is gone.

[5] On the leaf-impressed side, apply a base color in gold or light brown. Use the palette knife to add drops of other colors and mix lightly (**photo k**). Continue to add and remove color with the palette knife or a cotton swab until the leaf shape is defined and the composition is pleasing. Set colors with the heat gun, as in step 4. If a hue isn't deep enough or you want to add another color, additional layers of colors may be added after setting each with the heat gun.

Apply the backing

[1] Condition the black polymer clay (Basics) and run it through the pasta machine at a medium setting. Cut a backing layer, using a circle cutter slightly larger than your pendant.

[2] Wrap the black clay circle smoothly around the back. Trim it to form a neat border when viewed from the front (**photo l**).

[3] Texture the back with coarse sandpaper or a texturing sheet, or leave it smooth to be sanded and polished after baking.

Finish the pendant

[1] Bake the pendant for 30–40 minutes or follow the manufacturer's directions.

MATERIALS

- 1 oz. (28g) scrap polymer clay
- 2-oz. (56g) pkg. Sculpey SuperFlex Bake & Bend modeling compound, any color
- Premo Sculpey, 1 oz. (28g) each of the following colors: gold metallic and black
- leaf or other sprig of foliage
- 23K gold leaf
- Translucent Liquid Sculpey (TLS)
- Piñata Inks by Jacquard, several colors (jacquardproducts.com)
- 2-part epoxy resin finish
- 4-in. (10cm) length of 19-gauge gold wire
- **2–3** accent beads
- gold chain, 20–24 in. (51–61cm)

TOOLS & SUPPLIES

- pasta machine*
- toaster or convection oven*
- circle cutters
- tissue blade
- cornstarch
- rubber stamp, border design approximately ½ x 3 in. (1.3 x 7.6cm)
- soft-bristled brush
- glass or Plexiglas sheet for palette
- plastic palette knife
- heat gun (for embossing and crafts)
- cyanoacrylate glue gel
- roundnose pliers

*Dedicated to nonfood use

[2] Mix the two-part epoxy resin according to the directions. Pour a smooth layer of resin on the surface of the cooled pendant. Check for drips or bubbles. Be aware that most epoxies need several hours – some as many as 24 – to cure. Let the pendant dry in a dust-free area (such as inside a cupboard) to avoid contamination.

[3] Drill a hole in the top of the pendant. With roundnose pliers, make a wrapped-loop eye pin from gold wire. Add accent beads. Touch the tip of the eye pin to cyanoacrylate glue and embed it into the hole in the pendant. Allow to dry. Add the chain.

GOLD LEAF:

Genuine 23K gold leaf is more expensive than imitation leaf but proves a more cost-efficient choice in the long run. Actual gold leaf is easier to handle and control. It comes in 3 x 3-in. (7.6 x 7.6cm) sheets attached to a tissue paper carrier that can be trimmed with scissors. Use it sparingly.

Faux porcelain beads

Use polymer clay to make hollow beads
reminiscent of fine porcelain

by **Deborah Anderson**

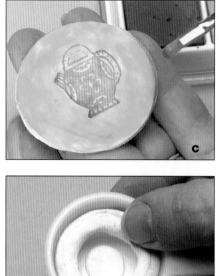

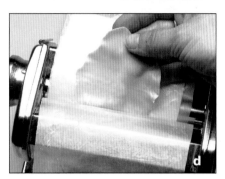

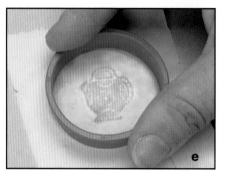

These dome- and cylinder-shaped polymer-clay beads look and feel like porcelain, but because they are hollow, they're lightweight. For domed beads similar to the ones shown here, transfer or stamp an image on one side and a word on the other. The cylinder beads contain almost narrative sequences of collages around their sides.

Although the transfer technique using translucent clay used here originated from Gwen Gibson's video "Ancient Images," experimentation with other products led to using Decorating Chalks by Craf-T Products. These colorfast, easy-to-use chalks should be applied with a paintbrush to color the clay after you've transferred an image. For stamping an image on the clay, Ancient Page ink pads are recommended because the ink is dye-based and dries quickly.

Decorate the clay
[1] Condition 1–2 oz. (28–56g) of white polymer clay (see Basics, p. 5).
[2] Run the clay through a pasta machine on a medium setting (1/16 in./2mm).
[3] Cut two circles from the sheet with a circle cutter; use whatever size you like, but make both pieces the same size.
[4] If you are using photocopied images, cut two images that will fit as you desire on the circles to transfer. Color them with colored pencils, if you wish.

[5] Place one image face down on each clay circle. Burnish several times over the course of at least a 15-minute period. Lift up a corner to see how dark the image is (**photo a**). If it needs to be darker, leave the paper on longer. Alternatively, you can ink a rubber stamp and stamp a design directly on the clay (**photo b**). Test the inked stamp on paper first to check for clarity. After you've stamped the clay, allow it to dry before proceeding.
[6] Apply Decorating Chalks with a brush to color the background if you wish (**photo c**).

Seal the images
[1] Condition 1–2 oz. (28–56g) of translucent polymer clay and run it through the pasta machine's thinnest setting (1/32 in./1mm).
[2] Place the sheet of translucent clay between two 5 x 5-in. (13 x 13cm) sheets of waxed paper and put the same size sheet of printer-weight paper underneath.
[3] With the pasta machine set at its thinnest setting, insert the layers between the rollers and run until the machine catches the clay's edge. Hold the clay sheet only and allow the papers to fall to either side. Run the layers through the pasta machine, holding onto the clay sheet only (**photo d**). This prevents the layers from buckling and curling as they pass through the rollers.
[4] Remove the top layer of waxed

paper from the clay. Pull the clay gently off the other piece of waxed paper and place it on a sheet of cardstock. You may need to cool it first in a refrigerator and use a tissue blade to ease removal.
[5] Place both white clay circles image side down on the thin translucent sheet. Gently press to affix them together, being careful not to trap air. Turn the piece so that the translucent clay is on top. You should be able to see the image through the translucent clay. Use the same circle cutter you used before to slice the translucent clay around the original circles (**photo e**).

Form the sphere-shaped bead
[1] Brush the image side of each circle with a little cornstarch. Place one circle, image side down, inside the round tablespoon-size measuring spoon. Put a slightly flattened, pea-size ball of white clay in the center of the circle.
[2] Roll a snake 1/8 in. (3mm) in diameter and rim the interior edge of the circle with it (**photo f**). Pop the piece out of the measuring spoon and repeat steps 1–2 with the other circle. You now have two domes.
[3] Put the two domes together and smooth the seams with your fingers (**photo g**). You now have a sphere.
[4] Use a needle tool to pierce a hole

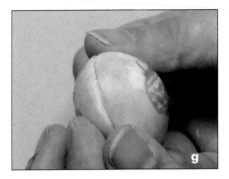

through each end (**photo h**).

[5] Place each bead on a piece of polyester batting on a cookie sheet. Bake at 250°F (120°C) for 1 hour and allow to cool.

[6] Place the baked bead in a container of water and wet-sand the bead, starting with 400-grit sandpaper and continuing with 600-grit. Rinse and dry. Polish with a cloth or use a buffer.

Form the cylinder-shaped bead

[1] Condition 1–2 oz. (28–56g) each of black, white, and translucent polymer clay. Run the black and white clays separately into sheets through the pasta machine set on the thickest setting.

[2] Cut a piece of white clay 2 x 1 in. (5 x 2.5cm).

[3] Repeat steps 4–6 of the "Decorate the clay" section on p. 90.

[4] Repeat steps 1–4 of the "Seal the images" section on p. 90 to prepare the translucent clay.

[5] Seal the white clay rectangle image side down on the translucent sheet of clay, taking care not to trap air. Use a tissue blade to trim the excess clay.

[6] Roll the clay rectangle into a cylinder and connect the seams (**photo i**). Hold your finger under the seam and rub to make it smooth. Press the cylinder into the desired shape.

[7] If you would like to have textured ends on your cylinder bead, place the sheet of black clay over a texturing sheet or a piece of screen. Roll a brayer or an acrylic rod over the clay to impress the pattern (**photo j**). Turn over and peel away the texturing sheet or screen. Turn the sheet over again so the textured side is face down.

[8] Place the cylinder on end on top of the black clay sheet. Press firmly to impress the edge of the cylinder (**photo k**) and carefully cut out the shape with a craft knife.

[9] Attach the black end cap on the cylinder by pressing gently. Smooth the seams but avoid marring any texture that has been applied (**photo l**).

[10] Repeat steps 8–9 for the cylinder's other end.

[11] Pierce the center of each end with a needle tool.

[12] Repeat steps 5–6 of the "Form the sphere-shaped bead" section above to complete the bead.

MATERIALS

- Fimo Soft, one 2-oz. (56g) pkg. each of the following colors: white, translucent, and black
- black-and-white photocopies and/or rubber stamps
- colored pencils
- Ancient Page ink pad (available at art supply and hobby shops)
- Craft-T Decorating Chalks

TOOLS & SUPPLIES

- pasta machine*
- toaster or convection oven*
- 1½-, 1¼-, or 1-in. (3.8, 3.2, or 2.5cm) circle cutters
- scissors
- bone folder or wooden knife for burnishing
- small paintbrush
- waxed paper
- photocopy or printer paper
- cardstock
- NuBlade
- cornstarch
- round tablespoon and teaspoon measuring spoons*
- needle tool
- craft knife and tissue blade
- brayer or acrylic rod
- 400- and 600-grit wet/dry sandpaper
- buffing machine or soft polishing cloth
- cookie sheet*
- polyester batting

*Dedicated to nonfood use

Faux stone

Can you wring stone from clay?
You can with polymer!

by **Patricia Kimle**

The colors, texture, and grain of this polymer-clay "granite" will fool the eye of all but the most discerning viewer. This project outlines how to make beads for a stunning necklace and earring set, but this technique is ideal for creating decorative objects as well.

Make the granite beads

[1] Cover your work surface with waxed paper. Use the large holes of a cheese grater to shred translucent polymer clay into small bits. Use the small holes to shred the white, black, and pink polymer clays onto the pile (photo a). Don't use the grater for food preparation once it's been in contact with polymer clay.

[2] Toss the clay to mix the colors. Sprinkle on about 1 teaspoon (5ml) of each color of embossing powder, if desired.

[3] With a palette knife, drizzle paint over the pile and toss to mix (photo b). Add paint until the bits of clay are mostly covered with paint (photo c). Allow the painted bits to dry.

[4] Drizzle Translucent Liquid Sculpey (TLS) over the pile and toss again until the mixture begins to stick together.

[5] Transfer the clay to a clean sheet of waxed paper and compress the pile into a loaf about 1¼ x 1¼ x 3 in. (3.2 x 3.2 x 7.6cm) (photo d). If you would like, use an acrylic sheet and rod to help compress and shape the loaf.

[6] Cut three slices from the loaf about ⅜ in. (1cm) thick (photo e). With fingers and/or acrylic tools, work the sides into slight curves. Cut out the center hole with a circle punch (photo f). These are the donut beads.

[7] Trim the remaining section of the loaf into a uniform cube, removing

thin slices from the sides until it is smooth and square (**photo g**).

[**8**] Cut the clay into eight equal cubes (**photo h**). Smooth and compress them as necessary. Pierce them diagonally through opposite corners with a needle tool. These are the cube beads.

[**9**] Bake the beads according to the manufacturer's directions. Let them cool.

[**10**] Wet-sand the beads starting with 220-grit paper and working through the finer grits until the surfaces are as smooth as possible. Finish with two or three thin coats of water-based varnish.

String the necklace

[**1**] Cut four 8-in. (20cm) lengths of beading wire for the connections between the three donut beads. String about 2 in. (5cm) of seed beads on each, sliding the beads to 1 in. (2.5cm) from the end of the wire.

[**2**] Wrap one wire through the hole in a donut. The seed beads should be just tight enough to prevent the strand from slipping over a corner. Add or remove beads as necessary.

[**3**] String a 6mm bead and a crimp bead over both ends of one wire and tighten the loop. Repeat with the

second wire, spacing it as shown (**photo i**). Crimp the crimp beads (see Basics, p. 5).

[**4**] String 1 in. (2.5cm) of seed beads on each wire, covering the short tails. String both strands through one cube.

[**5**] String 1 in. (2.5cm) of seed beads, a crimp bead, and a hematite bead on each wire. String 2 in. (5cm) of seed beads and make a loop around another donut, as before. Take each wire back through the 6mm bead and the crimp and tighten the beads (**photo j**). Crimp the crimp beads.

[**6**] Repeat to connect a cube and

j

k

l

m

donut to the other edge of the center donut.

[7] Cut one 12-in. (30cm) and one 4-in. (10cm) piece of beading wire. String 2 in. (5cm) of seed beads on each, sliding the beads to 1 in. (2.5cm) from the end. Repeat steps 2–3, looping the beads around the end donut.

[8] String 1 in. (2.5cm) of seed beads on each wire, covering the short tails. String a crimp bead over both wires and crimp it (**photo k**).

[9] String a cube bead over the long tail, hiding the end of the 4-in. (10cm) wire. String 1 in. (2.5cm) of seed beads, a 6mm bead, and 1 in. (2.5cm) of seed beads. Continue adding beads until your necklace is the desired length.

[10] String a crimp bead and half the clasp. Go back through the crimp and a few beads (**photo l**). Tighten the loop around the clasp and crimp the crimp bead.

[11] Repeat steps 7–10 to finish the other end of the necklace. These instructions and the materials listed yield a 23-in. (58cm) necklace; adjust if you prefer a longer or shorter necklace.

Make the earrings

[1] Cut two 5-in. (13cm) pieces of beading wire. String a crimp bead close to one end and go back through the crimp to form a small loop. Crimp the crimp bead

MATERIALS

- 2-oz. (56g) pkg. Premo Sculpey, translucent
- Premo Sculpey, marble-size balls of each of the following colors: white, black, and pale pink (white with a pinch of copper)
- Translucent Liquid Sculpey (TLS)
- embossing powders, white, black, and/or gold (optional)
- acrylic paint, pewter
- water-based varnish
- **18** 6mm hematite beads
- 25g Japanese cylinder beads
- **20** crimp beads
- clasp
- flexible beading wire, .014–.019
- pair of earwires

TOOLS & SUPPLIES

- pasta machine*
- toaster or convection oven*
- waxed paper
- cheese grater with coarse and fine holes*
- palette knife
- tissue blade
- ⅜-in. (1cm) circle cutter
- wet/dry sandpaper in 220-, 320-, 400-, and 600-grits
- acrylic sheet and rod (optional)
- chainnose or crimping pliers
- flush cutters

*Dedicated to nonfood use

and cut off the short wire tail.

[2] String four seed beads, a crimp, a cube, 1 in. (2.5cm) of seed beads, a 6mm bead, and 1 in. (2.5cm) of seed beads. Go back through the cube and the crimp (**photo m**). Tighten the loop and crimp the crimp bead.

[3] Make a second earring to match

the first. Open the loops on the earring wires (Basics) and attach each beaded component. Close the loops.

CONTRIBUTORS

Deborah Anderson is a founding member of the South Bay Polymer Clay Guild in San Jose, California. View her work at geocities.com/thousand_canes. Contact Deborah at 408-998-5303 or by e-mail at MarahA@aol.com.

Jody Bishel is a multimedia artist whose work can be viewed in the online gallery pbase.com/jody. Contact Jody by e-mail at jbishel@sbcglobal.net.

Mike Buesseler, a nationally-recognized polymer clay artist, demonstrates his techniques in two videos available from Gameplan (gameplanvideo.com): *The All Polymer Metallic Clays* and *Landscape Canes.*

Terry Lee Czechowski is a multimedia artist who has been making polymer-clay jewelry for more than 10 years. Contact Terry at 518-383-3769 or by e-mail, tlc@tlc-creation.com. View her jewelry and other art at tlc-creation.com.

Grant Diffendaffer uses polymer and precious metal clay to create beads, jewelry, vessels, and other items inspired by the beauty of the natural world. He exhibits and teaches around the United States and in Canada. View Grant's work and class schedules at diffendaffer.com. Contact him at 510-207-2604 or by e-mail at grant@diffendaffer.com.

Christi Friesen creates mixed media sculptures using polymer clay, glass, gemstones, pearls, found objects, acrylics, and more. View her work at cforiginals.com or e-mail her at Christi@cforiginals.com.

Lura Hatcher began working with polymer clay in the late 1980s and often modeled her work after glass or lampwork beads she admired. She's since added glass and metal-working to her repertoire, and enjoys blending these media with polymer clay. Contact Lura by e-mail at mushi_01@yahoo.com.

Sarajane Helm's polymer clay art is influenced by a lifelong interest in textile and clothing design. Contact Sarajane by e-mail, sarajane@polyclay.com, or visit her Web site, polyclay.com.

Janis Holler has more than 20 years' experience with polymer clay. She describes her work as mixed media because she likes to use a wide array of materials as counterpoints to the clay. Contact Janis at 970-532-3982 or by e-mail at locolobo@earthlink.net. View her work at locolobodesigns.com.

Donna Kato is the author of *The Art of Polymer Clay*, and she has released several videotapes on polymer-clay techniques through Mindstorm Productions. Visit Donna's Web site, prairiecraft.com, for more details about her books, videos, and polymer-clay products.

Patricia Kimle, author of *Polymer Clay Inspirations* (North Light Books), exhibits her work and teaches polymer-clay techniques around the country. More examples of her art can be found at kimledesigns.com. Contact Patti by e-mail at patti@kimledesigns.com.

Dotty McMillan uses polymer clay to create one-of-a-kind kaleidoscopes, vessels, boxes, and jewelry. View her work at alookingglass.homestead.com/dottykaleidoscopes. Contact Dotty at 951-780-4052 or e-mail dmcmillan01@earthlink.net.

Karen and Ann Mitchell are the authors of *Liquid Polymer Clay: Fabulous New Techniques for Making Jewelry and Home Accents*. Their jewelry has appeared in feature films, television, theatrical productions, and museum exhibits. Examples of their work can be seen at www.ankaradesigns.com. Contact them at 626-798-8491 or e-mail Ann@ankaradesigns.com.

Mari O'Dell, a retired high-school art teacher, now spends her time creating with polymer clay, gardening, and traveling. Contact her at 410-263-7149 or e-mail juanymari@aol.com.

Nancy Pollack lets the clay and the moment lead her designs and is delighted by the constant surprises she uncovers. View Nancy's polymer-clay jewelry, beads, and vases at npolyclay.home.comcast.net. Nancy's e-mail is npolyclay@comcast.net.

Lee Radtke has been working with polymer clay since 1991. She is a past president of the National Polymer Clay Guild and a member of the Mile High Polymer Clay Guild in Denver. Contact her at 720-565-2554 or by e-mail at lradtke1@comcast.net.

Nan Roche is the author of *The New Clay* (Flower Valley Press, 1991). She teaches her techniques around the country and on television. Nan also has produced two polymer-clay videos. Contact her by e-mail at roche@helix.nih.gov. Nan would like to thank Tory Hughes for teaching her the techniques of

sanding and polishing and Esther Anderson and Patricia Echeagaray for inspiring her to try extruding *mokume gane*. She also thanks Carl Hornberger for the idea to adapt a caulking gun to extrude the clay and Jean Reist Stark and Josephine Reist Smith for their inspiring book, *Classical Loop-In-Loop Chains and Their Derivatives*.

Carly Seibel makes polymer beads, bead sets, and finished jewelry. Her work is displayed at geocities.com/lubellebeads. Contact Carly at 520-888-9092 or by e-mail at lubellebeads@yahoo.com

Sarah Shriver has been working with polymer clay for nearly 20 years. She teaches and speaks about her art at seminars and shows worldwide. Contact Sarah at 415-456-7335 or through her Web site, sarahshriver.com.

Aya Teshima has been drawn to and inspired by the ornate designs produced during the colorful era of King Kalakaua of Hawaii in the late 19th century. This interest is a return to her childhood wish to emulate the work of her great-grandfather, Maximillian, who was a goldsmith and jeweler during that time. Contact Aya at MauiPipkin@cs.com

Vicki J. Wulwick specializes in polymer-clay evening bags and boxes that use her innovative chain technique. View her work at polymerdragonfly.com or contact Vicki at vwulwick@polymerdragonfly.com.

Carol Zilliacus is an award-winning artist whose work is exhibited nationally in American Craft Council shows as well as Washington, D. C. area galleries. Her polymer-clay paintings, sculptures, and jewelry are inspired and influenced by both watercolor painting and a love of textiles. View her work at carolzilliacusartist.com or contact Carol at carolz32@comcast.net.

RESOURCES

Beadandbutton.com serves a community of beaders around the world who exchange ideas through the Beader's Forum. Visit the Polymer Clay forum for tips, techniques, resources, and discussions about this versatile medium.

Glassattic.com is an online reference source compiled by artist Diane Black. It covers hundreds of topics relating to polymer clay, including definitions, lessons, projects, and techniques.

NPCG.org is the official Web site of the National Polymer Clay Guild. It is full of articles and information, including a stunning gallery of members' art. It also provides links to local guilds and details for local workshops and classes.

Pcpolyzine.com is a Web-based magazine that features articles, projects, and book reviews. The site also includes industry news and announcements and a calendar of events.

Polymerclaycentral.com is a Web site with an abundance of information for artists, from beginner through advanced. The site is loaded with tips, projects, chat areas, and message boards. Monthly contests and challenges both hone skills and provide inspiration.

Polymerclaydaily.com is a blog devoted to polymer-clay art. It provides information, inspiration, and links to other artists.

MERCHANTS

Polymer clay products and tools are available at most craft or hobby stores. Additionally, try the following:

The Clay Factory, Inc., clayfactoryinc.com or (877) 728-5739, is an online store that offers products, tools, and accessories.

Kemper Enterprises, Inc., kempertools.com or (909) 627-6191, manufactures handcrafted, custom tools for the ceramic arts, including sculpting, molding, and cutting tools.

Polymer Clay Express, polymerclayexpress.com or (800) 844-0138, is an online store that offers a variety of clays, tools, accessories, and embellishments.

Poly-Tools, Inc., poly-tools.com, sells custom polymer-clay tools including bead rollers and slicers. Additionally, the site provides links to bead-making tutorials.

Prairie Craft Company, prairiecraft.com or (800) 779-0615, sells polymer clay and clay tools made or endorsed by artist Donna Kato. The online store sells a wide variety of products in addition to providing tutorials and tips.